Twayne's United States Authors Series

Sylvia E. Bowman, *Editor*

INDIANA UNIVERSITY

Gertrude Stein

TUSAS 268

Gertrude Stein

GERTRUDE STEIN

By MICHAEL J. HOFFMAN
University of California, Davis

GEORGE PRIOR PUBLISHERS
London, England

TWAYNE PUBLISHERS
A Division of G. K. Hall & Co.
Boston, Massachusetts, U. S. A.
1976

Library of Congress Cataloging in Publication Data
Hoffman, Michael J 1939-
  Gertrude Stein.

  (Twayne's United States authors series ; TUSAS
268)
  Bibliography: p. 147 - 53.
  Includes index.
  1. Stein, Gertrude, 1874-1946.
PS3537.T323Z655   818'.5'209   76-2661
ISBN 0-8057-7168-9

MANUFACTURED IN THE UNITED STATES OF AMERICA

For Diane

Contents

About the Author

Michael Hoffman's teaching career began in 1962 at Washington College, Chestertown, Maryland. In 1964 he joined the English Department at the University of Pennsylvania, where he had received his A.B. in 1959 and his Ph.D. in 1963. He stayed at Pennsylvania until 1967, when he left to teach at the University of California, Davis, where he is now Professor of English and has been chairman of the Graduate Program. He spent 1972-73 as a visiting professor of American literature at the Sorbonne. He is now Assistant to the Vice Chancellor of Academic Affairs at Davis.

This is Michael Hoffman's fourth book. His first, *The Development of Abstractionism in the Writings of Gertrude Stein*, was published in 1966 by the University of Pennsylvania Press. In 1971 he published a novel, *The Buddy System*, with Holt, Rinehart, & Winston, which also appeared as a Berkeley Medallion paperback. The Kennikat Press published his study of American Romanticism, *The Subversive Vision: American Romanticism in Literature* in 1973. Professor Hoffman's fiction and essays have appeared in a number of journals. He is now working on a book on Modernism as a sequel to *The Subversive Vision*.

Hoffman, who was born in 1939, is married and the father of four children. His wife, Diane, is a pianist and music teacher.

Preface

John Malcolm Brinnin has said that, "If Gertrude Stein had never lived, sooner or later works very much like those she produced would have been written by someone else. Once a particular set of conditions was present, her arrival was inevitable — like an event in chemistry."[1] In one sense, all writers are historically inevitable; the good ones are, of course, much more than that. The recurrent problem which critics have had in dealing with so eccentric a figure as Gertrude Stein has been to decide just how much more than that she is. With her centennial behind us, it is clear that she is a major name in twentieth-century letters, but is she also a major writer? That Stein's name has appeared on more than forty volumes of her own composition will not in itself insure her continued reputation. But when we couple that fact with her many literary, musical, and artistic friendships; with the controversy that has always surrounded her work; with her uncontested influence on a number of important writers; and with the fact that most of her works are still in print, then it is apparent that she is a figure of more than minor dimensions.

My contention is that Gertrude Stein is a major writer historically and intrinsically and that she has written some of the finest and most complex books of our time. Because the years 1902 and 1913 were her most prolific and innovative, as well as the most influential on the development of Modernism, I have devoted half this book to the writings of that decade, particularly *Three Lives,* the "portraits," *The Making of Americans,* and *Tender Buttons.* Through detailed analyses, I have tried to show how Stein's celebrated abstract style developed through a series of progressive stages from Realism to Cubism.

In the chapters that follow, I have analyzed more selectively the period from 1914 until Stein's death in 1946, a period during which she contributed to many different literary forms, such as the opera *Four Saints in Three Acts* and the novel *Lucy Church Amiably;* wrote her works of aesthetic theory, such as "Composition as Explanation" and *Lectures in America;* and composed the series of memoirs and autobiographies on which her current reputation is largely based, the most famous of these being *The Autobiography of Alice B. Toklas.* It is not possible in a book of this size to deal with all of Stein's writing, for the number of titles in the most recent census of her work numbers nearly six hundred,[2] ranging in length from portraits of half a dozen lines to a novel of 925 pages *(The Making of Americans).* I have chosen to concentrate on those items of most historical and intrinsic significance and to leave out the ones that seemed to repeat with neither interesting nor significant variations experiments already made and patterns already established in Stein's other work.

Throughout the book, I have attempted to place Stein within the context of the *avant-garde* movements of the first fifty years of twentieth-century literature and painting, for that is the only way in which her achievement can be adequately measured. Also, although I have had to be selective in dealing with the enormous mass of Stein's published writings, I have still treated most of what is the largest corpus written by any major author of our time. I hope I have offered the reader a detailed and comprehensive exposition, as well as a grounding in one of the important streams of Modernist culture.

MICHAEL J. HOFFMAN

University of California, Davis

Acknowledgments

I should like to thank the following for allowing me to quote from copyrighted and unpublished material written by Gertrude Stein:

The Estate of Gertrude Stein, for *A Long Gay Book*, in *Matisse Picasso and Gertrude Stein* (Paris: Plain Edition, 1932); *The Making of Americans* (Paris: Contact Editions, 1925). The Beinecke Rare Book and Manuscript Library, Yale University, for permission to make use of the unpublished manuscript, "American Language and Literature."

Random House, Inc., for *Lectures in America*, copyright 1935 by Random House, Inc.; and *Portraits and Prayers*, copyright 1934 by the Modern Library, Inc.

Diana Hoffman and Elaine Bukhari have read, typed, and helped very much to edit the manuscript, and I thank them both. My earlier debts with relation to Gertrude Stein have been acknowledged in the preface to *The Development of Abstractionism in the Writings of Gertrude Stein* (1966). Since that time Professor Richard Bridgman's indispensable book, *Gertrude Stein in Pieces* (1970), has forced me to reassess all my previous ideas about Stein. I am deeply indebted to him.

The University of California, Davis, deserves thanks for providing me with ideal teaching and research conditions. I have benefited from grants-in-aid given by the Committee on Research as well as from summer research grants given by the Humanities Institute of the University of California.

My personal thanks go to Professor James Woodress for his continuous interest in my work and to my wife Diane for a thousand small encouragements too numerous to recall. Because of her, this is a better book than I could otherwise have written.

Chronology

1874 Gertrude Stein born, February 3, in Allegheny, Pennsylvania.
1875 - Stein family lives in Austria and France.
1878
1877 Alice Toklas born, April 30, in San Francisco.
1879 Stein family lives in Baltimore.
1880 Stein family moves to Oakland. Lives in various houses throughout decade. Stein's father makes money in San Francisco street railways.
1888 Stein's mother, Amelia, dies.
1891 Her father, Daniel, dies. Her brother Michael takes over as head of family. They move to San Francisco.
1892 Stein goes to live in Baltimore.
1893 Enters Harvard Annex (renamed Radcliffe College the following year).
1894 Works under Hugo Münsterberg in Harvard Psychological Laboratory.
1896 Publishes "Normal Motor Automatism," with Leon Solomons in *Psychological Review*. Her first publication.
1897 Enters Johns Hopkins Medical School.
1901 Fails four courses at Hopkins. Does not receive degree.
1903 Settles with brother Leo at 27, rue de Fleurus, Paris. Writes *Q. E. D.* and begins *The Making of Americans*.
1905 Begins *Three Lives*. She and Leo purchase Henri Matisse's *La Femme au Chapeau* at the Salon d'Automne. Meets Pablo Picasso.
1906 Poses for Picasso portrait. Finishes *Three Lives*. Returns to work on *The Making of Americans*.
1907 Alice Toklas arrives in Paris.
1909 Alice moves into the apartment at the rue de Fleurus. *Three Lives* published. First book.

1911	Finishes *The Making of Americans.*
1912	"Matisse" and "Picasso" published in Alfred Stieglitz's *Camera Work.*
1913	The Armory Show opens in New York. First exhibition of Modernist painting in the United States. Leo moves out.
1914	*Tender Buttons* published.
1917	Drives a Ford van, "Auntie," for American Fund for French Wounded.
1921	Meets Sherwood Anderson.
1922	Meets Ernest Hemingway. *Geography and Plays* published.
1924	Parts of *The Making of Americans* serialized in Ford Madox Ford's *transatlantic review.*
1925	*The Making of Americans* published.
1926	Lectures on "Composition as Explanation" at Oxford and Cambridge. Meets Virgil Thomson.
1928	Basket I, the poodle, arrives.
1929	She and Alice lease house at Bilignin.
1931	*The Plain Edition* begins publication in January with *Lucy Church Amiably.*
1932	Writes *The Autobiography of Alice B. Toklas.*
1933	*The Autobiography* is published and becomes a bestseller.
1934	*Four Saints in Three Acts* opens in Hartford, and then goes to New York. Stein lectures in United States.
1935	Lecture series continues. She and Alice return to France in May.
1936	Lectures again at Oxford and Cambridge.
1938	She and Alice move to rue Christine.
1939	They close Paris apartment because of war and move to Bilignin.
1943	Move to Culoz, near Bilignin.
1944	Occupation ends. Stein meets American soldiers. She and Alice return to Paris in December.
1945	They tour American Army bases in occupied Germany. Stein lectures in Brussels.
1946	She dies of cancer, July 27.
1947	Leo dies.
1967	Alice Toklas dies.

CHAPTER 1

Introduction

I *The Paradoxes of Gertrude Stein*

TO write about Gertrude Stein is to plunge immediately into paradox. For one thing, the simple mention of her name still arouses extremes of adulation or ridicule. She is considered by most people the chief modern literary eccentric. And yet, there are many — some of them grudgingly — who consider her a major author, the founder of a new literary style, the great apologist for Modernism, and the discoverer and promoter of the French school of contemporary painting. She was hated and loved during her lifetime, and more than a quarter century after her death she continues to evoke the same divided response. But, if the above paradoxes are not enough, it is even more ironic that, despite her large; contradictory reputation, very few people have read Stein's work. Even literary academics rarely venture beyond *Three Lives* and *The Autobiography of Alice B. Toklas,* and the great mass of the educated reading public can do little more than quote "Pigeons in the grass alas" and "A rose is a rose is a rose is a rose," usually forgetting the last rose.

"It always did bother me," she lamented late in her career, "that the American public were more interested in me than in my work"[1]; but the reasons for this paradox were largely her own fault, and we wonder just how sincerely she complained. She was conscious throughout her career of the value of public relations, and she finally became her own publicist during the 1930s when both the great success of *The Autobiography of Alice B. Toklas* and her subsequent triumphal tour of the United States turned her into one of the best-known writers in the English language. She had the good fortune to meet many of this century's leading painters when she arrived in Paris during the early 1900s; and she had both the prescience to recognize their value while they were still unknown and the good sense to remain publicly connected with them during the course of her long expatriation.

Her name was constantly associated with Henri Matisse and Pablo Picasso in the early years and with F. Scott Fitzgerald, Sherwood Anderson, and Ernest Hemingway in the halcyon 1920s. Hemingway did the greatest service to her reputation by including her reputed statement about the "lost generation" as an epigraph to *The Sun Also Rises*. When her work was first read on any large scale, she was a woman of almost sixty; and she was known by that time primarily as the writer of quirky memoirs of wicked artistic life in Paris. By then, it was all too easy to sidestep her truly innovative work; readers could now serve their obligation to "*avant-garde*" literature by reading one of Stein's quite accessible "autobiographies." In fact, it hardly mattered whether readers read her or not, for she was by that time an almost mythical literary force whose magnitude surpassed anything she ever wrote, a literary demigod to whose Parisian sanctuary the world came to pay tribute.

Being a person of definite tastes and of a certain immobility of character, she aroused in others every extreme of rapture and indignation, especially in those who knew her well. Her brother Leo thought her a charlatan,[2] but artists as diverse as Picasso and Anderson praised her as one of the great contemporary innovators.[3] Hemingway originally shared the latters' feelings, but he soon thought better of his discipleship and disavowed her influence, just as he had turned on Anderson in *The Torrents of Spring*. Hemingway's literary ingratitude is by now legendary; but, given Stein's stolid peremptoriness, we can scarcely blame him. Certain statements in *The Autobiography of Alice B. Toklas* indicate something of Stein's manner. She recalls dismissing Ezra Pound after he fell out of one of her Renaissance chairs, and she says contemptuously of Glenway Wescott that "He has a certain syrup but it does not pour."[4] But, with all her imperial style and cutting wit, she was loved affectionately by many people — among them Thornton Wilder and Virgil Thomson[5] — who found her warm, wise, and understanding. Certainly for American soldiers in both world wars she was literally a mother away from home.

With her centenary behind us, the extremes are still reflected in print. Donald Sutherland, who knew her, wrote in *Gertrude Stein: A Biography of Her Work* (1951)[6] a brilliant, eccentric, and thoroughly personal defense of a woman whom he obviously judged to be the great writer of her time. By contrast, B. L. Reid, who did not know her, published seven years later an equally cranky book[7] that was designed to read Stein out of the literary pantheon. Even in the mid-1960s Kingsley Widmer was able to dismiss her as a "shrewd self-publicist" and as an "*avant-kitsch* writer."[8] The controversy will no doubt continue.

Anyone, therefore, who wishes to come to terms with what Stein was actually trying to do in her writing must attempt to distinguish between the work and the reputation — a task that is not at all easy. Until quite recently, entirely too much print has been wasted in a spirit of partisanship by those who have wished to prove Stein either a fraud or a genius. Even in his stimulating and perceptive critical biography, *The Third Rose*,[9] John Malcolm Brinnin exhibits continuous piqued disapproval of many of his subject's attitudes and of much of her behavior. Indeed, only in the past decade have the first attempts at dispassionate examination appeared. My earlier study, *The Development of Abstractionism in the Writings of Gertrude Stein*,[10] and Allegra Stewart's *Gertrude Stein and the Present*[11] appeared, respectively, in 1966 and 1967; and they were followed in 1970 by Norman Weinstein's *Gertrude Stein and the Literature of Modern Consciousness*[12] and by Richard Bridgman's distinguished *Gertrude Stein in Pieces*,[13] the first full-length treatment of the entire Stein canon. In 1974 appeared James Mellow's fine, sympathetic biography, *Charmed Circle: Gertrude Stein & Company*,[14] and it superseded (as a life but not as criticism) Brinnin's *The Third Rose*. It is now possible to approach Stein outside a spirit of polemic, a fact that has been made clear by the number of both doctoral dissertations and popular biographies that have taken Stein for their subject.[15]

The next paradox is that, although Stein was by education a child of nineteenth-century science, she was by later achievement a founder and chief purveyor of Modernism. As a Radcliffe undergraduate in the middle 1890s, she was trained in the Harvard psychology laboratory under William James and Hugo Münsterberg, from whom she learned the contemporary theories of personality. She conducted original research with a graduate student, Leon Solomons, on problems of attention and automatic writing, publishing the results of that work in two articles in *The Psychological Review*.[16] Continuing her education at the Johns Hopkins Medical School, she did research on the physiology of the brain; but she left after four years without taking her degree, having done badly in her final year and having, as she tells us in Alice Toklas's "autobiography," simply lost interest in medicine.[17]

At this point she was not sure what she really wanted to do other than realize an ambition both she and Leo had held since they were children — to achieve *la gloire;*[18] but she knew that she did not wish to spend a lifetime delivering babies. She traveled for a few years, finally settling in Paris with Leo at 27 rue de Fleurus where she lived most of the rest of her life as a woman of limited but independent means. Alice Toklas arrived in 1907; and, although Leo remained until around 1913, his relationship with Gertrude was quite strained for a few years before that. But, by the time of Alice, the Stein atelier was well known among Paris artists; and Saturday nights at the rue de Fleurus were an occasion. For a long time, Leo Stein occupied center stage; for most of the company was unaware that Gertrude had begun to write. With steady, quiet persistence, she composed *Q. E. D., Three Lives,* and *The Making of Americans* before more than a handful of people knew what she was doing. It was only after her work began to be noticed that her brother's ascendancy waned. The lapsed scientist and medical student had already done much of the writing that was to create the new shape of twentieth-century literature.

While this development may seem at first a strange turn of circumstance, it is quite easy through hindsight to see the beginnings of Stein's characteristic theories of personality in the second of her articles, "Cultivated Motor Automatism," a suggestion she herself made in *Lectures in America.*[19] I shall consider this matter in the next chapter while discussing her early novella *Q. E. D.* (published for the first time in 1950 as *Things as They Are*).[20] The implied theory she presents in that article — that one can discover the secret of human personality by somehow isolating and describing all discernible personality types — dominated her entire creative life, especially the earliest and most inventive part of her career. This emphasis on personality types is a belief she shares with both the psychological theorists of the later nineteenth century and with other writers who came of age at the same time, writers as diverse as Theodore Dreiser and Lincoln Steffens.[21]

II *The Development of Modernism*

Although we tend to think of her as primarily a stylist, Stein shared with the so-called Naturalists a deep-rooted psychological determinism. This statement in itself tells us little about her essential qualities as a writer, however, for the radical assumptions she held about narrative structure enabled her to go beyond any of her fellow determinists. Dreiser, for instance, always seems to treat his characters with the kind of yearning sentimentalism that we feel with Sister Carrie as she broods in her rocking chair or with Jennie Gerhardt as she stands isolated at her lover's funeral. At the end of the Romantic century, writers like Dreiser, Jack London, and Frank Norris found no meaning at all in the world beyond absolute cosmic necessity and the unavoidable violation of the individual. These attitudes are implicit in the Romantic world view that divine and social sanctions no longer apply in a mechanistically oriented and biologically determined universe. The great contribution of the new art that Stein represents is the belief that, even though humankind can not escape the philosophical dilemma inherent in determinism, it is still possible — in fact, necessary — to find ways to create works of art that transcend the sentimentality inherent in nihilistic despair. For stylists like Stein, the grounds of violation must be shifted from the individual to the very structure and texture of the work of art itself.

It was Henry James who began tentatively to explore this new task of the novel in English. His great later works — *The Ambassadors, The Wings of the Dove,* and *The Golden Bowl* — continue to present his earlier vision that the individual must renounce the world in order to go on living morally in a universe without God; but, instead of merely repeating himself and being backed finally into the *cul-de-sac* of sentimental despair, he shifts the grounds of his attention and disorientation away from the individual character to a style whose limits he extends to a point just short of fragmentation. He progressively minimizes the "realistic" texture of detail and of social context in order to concentrate on the individual consciousness as it comes to terms not only with the world and with itself but with moral problems that become almost totally abstracted from the social milieu in which they first arose. As much, however, as James strived for a new vision, he was not willing finally to tamper with either the temporal or spatial orders of his narrative. But Stein and Joyce, Picasso and Matisse, Arnold Schönberg and Igor Stravinsky, Ezra Pound and T. S. Eliot were. James, Paul Cézanne, and Gustav Mahler had reached the limits of the old conventions. There was nothing left for the twentieth-century artist but to fragment the structures through which he had always found "reality" presented in order to reconstruct the world anew.

At the end of an old vision, innovators during the first decade of our century brought into being artistic, scientific, and philosophical revolutions as drastic as any since the Renaissance. But no development was more drastic than the realization that the structures within which artists had worked, within which it had for centuries been assumed they *had* to work, were nothing more than conventions that were traditionally accepted without question. The implicit challenges posed by the work of such artists as Picasso, however, spelled doom for the Renaissance tradition of painterly composition. Why must artists paint within the "laws" of perspective? Why are they beholden to any so-called "rules" of imitation? Matisse raised the same kinds of doubts about the traditional uses in painting of colors and of three-dimensional space. Cézanne had shown painters it was more important to discover the geometric structures underlying objects than to reproduce these objects exactly: James had demonstrated that form is an integral function in the moral argument of fiction. It was only another step to the realization that artists were not bound by *any* externally imposed necessity, and that, moreover, they never had been. With this new freedom, artists could now create forms of their own choosing. While this loosening of the aesthetic chains is still threatening to many people and while it has permitted a great deal of charlatanism, it has also enabled artists to create a new vision of the world. The great proliferation of Modernist masterpieces during the first decades of this century is ample evidence of the release of energy provided by the new vision.

Gertrude Stein, like so many of her contemporaries, wished her work to escape from its traditional dependence on the "real world" into a completely self-contained existence. The only way for a work of art to become truly autonomous, however, is for it to renounce all mimetic aspiration. That this rejection is basically unattainable has not deterred painters from Picasso to Jackson Pollock from attempting the impossible. Stein's aspirations are quite the same: she wishes her writings to create worlds with their own — not "reality's" — senses of internal coherence and rigid necessity.

Some implicit questions about narrative that Stein was among the first to suggest are: What is so sacred about the continuous-narrative structure? Why must the writer follow a linear time sequence in telling a tale? Why does narrative development have to follow the dramatic metaphor? Her first full-length belletristic attempt was a Jamesian novella based on a conception of personality as a static entity and on a vision that is psychologically deterministic; but the story is saved from its potential for nihilistic sentimentality by two elements: 1) its carefully worked-out geometric structure, and 2) its emphasis on the individual consciousness rather than on the entrapment of characters in inexorable situations. With "Melanctha," the

great central tale in *Three Lives,* Stein for the first time took a
genuine step away from narrative and linguistic conventions by ex-
hibiting the earliest trappings of her "abstract" style and by conceiv-
ing the narrative continuity of her story in nonlinear terms.
Therein lies yet another paradox. How does Stein move within just
a few years from a stylized Jamesian realism to both a fragmented
narrative structure and a ritualized style, and then, within less than a
decade, turn to a use of language in which words cease to be
purveyors of conventional meaning and become plastic counters to
be manipulated purely in obedience to the artist's expressive will,
just as painters manipulate nonsemantic line and color? Is there
anything in her earliest work and in her background to prefigure this
shift? It is an important question; for, if Stein can be described as an
abstractionist, then it is also true that she was not always an abstractionist. She became one steadily and progressively, moving through
a series of stylistic shifts as fascinating to observe as any similar
odyssey in twentieth-century art. Stein shared with other Modernists
the almost obsessive notion that artists never repeat themselves;
that, as soon as they explore and conquer a particular problem of
their craft, they must move on to confront and solve another one.
Picasso moves from blue to rose to Fauve to Cubist periods within
the space of four or five years. Joyce, moving in the semantically opposite direction from Stein, nonetheless passes through a similar
development of his allusionist style, resolutely refusing to repeat
himself from one work to another. It was Ezra Pound's constant cry
that the poet must "make it new." And Stein herself was to say many
times, "If you can do something, why do it?"[22]

III   *Toward a Definition of Abstractionism*

But, if we are to talk about Stein's progressive abstractionism, our
first task is to find a critical language with which to describe it.
Because most writers — even Joyce — stay within generally accepted narrative conventions, we can write comfortably about their
works with a language that consists of such traditional terms as sym-
bol, character, plot, imagery, and myth. But it quickly becomes clear
that Stein affords critics progressively fewer opportunities to use
such concepts. By the time we reach *Tender Buttons* (1913), we are
left with little more to talk about than English syntax and Stein's
violations of it. If we wish to go farther and discuss the analogies of
Tender Buttons with Cubist painting or with mystical experience,
we are forced to import categories external to the text.

In order to develop a language adequate to deal with Stein's writing, I developed in my first book the following concept of abstractionism:

> Among the definitions of the noun "abstraction" on page eight of Webster's *Third International Unabridged Dictionary* appears the following: "The act or process of leaving out of consideration one or more qualities of a complex object so as to attend to others." Under this definition we can subsume, for all practical purposes, the characteristics of abstractionism that appear in the early writings of Gertrude Stein. Her writings, almost from the very beginning, are characterized in style and subject matter by a progressive "leaving-out" of elements normally appearing in the works of most of her American contemporaries and immediate European predecessors. In terms of the "complex object" of realistic verisimilitude, for instance, Gertrude Stein from the beginning left out the small detail and careful description of externals that the realists had long used to convey the illusion of reality. . . . The first effect of this "art by subtraction," then, is the loss of the traditional verisimilitude of the realistic novel.[23]

But there are other examples of Stein's abstractionism, and one of these is her disavowal of the transparent narrator. From the beginning she never accepted Stephen Dedalus's metaphor of the artist as "the God of the creation," who "remains within or behind or beyond or above his handiwork, invisible, refined out of existence, indifferent, paring his fingernails."[24] As author-narrator, she intrudes repeatedly throughout the length of the story; she states her self-conscious thoughts at whatever moment they arise in her consciousness. As a result, by the time of *The Making of Americans*, she has sacrificed almost all her speed of narrative flow. In addition, there is scant physical movement within her fictional world; therefore, very little "happens" in a Stein tale: "People talk, they are described, we see them change subtly. But the closer she moved toward her descriptions of the 'essences' of people and things, as in the portraits and *Tender Buttons*, the less she felt she had to make people and things 'do'; they merely had to 'be'."[25]

We can point to other aspects of Stein's "art by subtraction," such as her use of abrupt juxtaposition and ritualistic repetition as well as her idiosyncratic punctuation and capitalization. Also, we must contend with her willingness to include much thoroughly private information in her compositions, much as Pound and Joyce are to do, particularly in *The Cantos* and in *Finnegans Wake*, respectively. What I should like to stress now is that we must be prepared to look for the ways in which Stein progressively abstracted from her writing most of the traditional elements of fictional prose narrative. When her work is juxtaposed to that of the major novelists of her time — novelists as diverse as Dreiser and Joseph Conrad — Stein's "abstractionism" should be quite apparent.

CHAPTER 2

The Beginnings

I Q. E. D.

A SIDE from a long passage entitled "Fernhurst", later rewritten as part of *The Making of Americans,* Stein's first sustained and completed piece of fiction was *Q. E. D.*, a novella she finished in October 1903. This almost totally autobiographical story was not published until 1950 when it appeared in a limited edition with the title *Things as They Are,*[1] which was taken from a line near the end of the text. Like most of her early works, Stein's first tale had to wait many years for publication.

To those concerned with the author's life, *Q. E. D.* affords the opportunity to see Stein treat the kinds of subject matter and emotion that she was henceforth to abolish from her writing. The story is about a homosexual triangle among three young American women,[2] but the focus is not on lesbianism *per se.* Rather, Stein deals with the shifting grounds of interpersonal relationships and with the tortured mental and emotional convolutions of a character named Adele who is modeled after Gertrude Stein herself and who functions as the story's central consciousness. That Stein was sensitive to the emotional self-exposure of this early work is evidenced by the fact that she seems to have forgotten it almost totally; she excised it from her life until 1932 when she rediscovered it and asked at the time, "Was it hidden with intention?"[3] The question is obviously rhetorical; for, in the many books that were to follow *Q. E. D.*, the author disappears behind a protective mask made possible by the form and style she discovered in *Three Lives.*

Q. E. D. seems quite old-fashioned after Stein's later work. It presents stylistic difficulties, and the narrative progression is linear. Chronological time proceeds without breaks or shifts or the unusual temporal juxtapositions that appear for the first time in "Melanctha." A reading of *Q. E. D.* will dispel the notion that Stein was incapable of telling a straightforward tale in conventional English. The tradition into which this old-fashioned novella fits is one I have loosely called Jamesian, and I imply with this term a contrast with the Naturalistic novel as it is represented in Europe, for example, by Emile Zola and in the United States by Theodore Dreiser. Phillip Rahv has suggested that the essence of Naturalism is a determinism controlled by the author's use of background and setting to imply the absolute, external determination of a character's fate.[4] I have previously suggested that Stein is a determinist, but her determinism is not controlled by a heavy use of background and setting; it is psychological, and it arises from her theory of human personality types. In order for Dreiser to render an event, he must reproduce a scene down to the very clothing his characters wear; for him, fact and reality are absolutely identical. In James, however, although he always had at least a selective interest in setting and physical description, the main narrative focus is on the interaction of consciousnesses as his characters struggle with their moral dilemmas.

Stein had almost certainly not read Dreiser, for at that time most copies of *Sister Carrie* were sitting in the Doubleday warehouse. Alice Toklas's persona asserts that Gertrude Stein had not read Henry James during her formative years.[5] But the evidence in *Q. E. D.* gives the lie to that contention, for Adele mentions Kate Croy by name when comparing herself to that member of the triangle in *The Wings of the Dove*.[6] Stein goes even farther than James; she finally abolishes setting almost completely to concentrate on Adele's consciousness and on the shiftings of power among the three women.

The figure of the triangle is a key to *Q. E. D.*, and the suggestions of plane geometry in the title give an index to Stein's intentions. There are three characters: Adele (whose family name we are not told), Mabel Neathe, and Helen Thomas who is the love object for the other two and thereby the source of the story's tension. The triangularity of the book's structure is almost obsessive. There are three books, each one named after a side of the triangle. The girls, financially independent in the Jamesian tradition, take three trips to Europe. The elapsed calendar time of the tale is three years, with the second the high point for Adele and Helen, after which Mabel finally wins control of the latter. Stein creates three distinct personality types. Adele is slow, talkative, straightforward, and sensual; Mabel is prudish, hard, and calculating; Helen is passionate and headstrong, but easily controlled by others. The emphasis on geometric figures and demonstration is an outgrowth of Stein's scientific background; for, while the novel's structure functions on the metaphor of plane geometry, its matter is "the demonstration of a proof of certain theorems on the subject of personality."[7]

In her second article, "Cultivated Motor Automatism,"[8] Stein expressed her overriding interest in psychological types; and her enthusiasm was clearly more a creative artist's than a scientist's. Fascinated by the students who came to the laboratory to attempt automatic writing, she was indifferent to the results of her experiments. In describing her subjects, she divides them into such types as the following: "A large number of my subjects were New Englanders, and the habit of self-repression, the intense self-consciousness, the morbid fear of 'letting one's self go,' that is so prominent an element in the New England character, was a constant stumbling-block."[9]

Five years later, Stein developed a character strikingly similar to this abstraction in Mabel Neathe, who has a "long angular body" that "betrayed her New England origin" (4). After Stein invokes this description, everything Mabel does in the book is directly consistent with the characteristics implied by her type. These typological considerations, prefigured in the article, continue as a distinctive pattern throughout Stein's career. She states a typological description and then feels she has fixed the character forever in his mold. As she was to say in *The Making of Americans*, "It is hard living down the tempers we are born with."[10]

With such a monolithic conception of personality, it is no wonder that, from the beginning, Stein's narratives notably lack the kinds of character change that have been a chief convention of fiction. Since her characters can neither change nor hope to change, she focuses our attention on the ways in which they finally accept their fates. There is something classically ritualistic in this, but Stein's emphasis on psychological determination in a world devoid of universal moral truth is anything but classical.

At the end of three years in *Q. E. D.;* after trips to Europe, to Baltimore, to New York; after secret letters to and assignations with Helen; and after struggles with her own conscience, Adele has gotten no farther than she was at the beginning. She is unable either to accept a permanent relationship with Helen or to win her away from the dominant Mabel. At the end, Adele curses Helen's inability to distinguish between illusion and reality: " 'Can't she see things as they are and not as she would make them if she were strong enough as she plainly isn't' "(133). But the question solves nothing, and Adele drops her head on her hands, saying as the book closes, " 'I am afraid it comes very near being a dead-lock.' "

It is of course a deadlock, just as it has been all along. Because Stein believes that every individual's inner consciousness is determined at birth, she deals scarcely at all with the personal backgrounds of her characters. None of them — except for Helen Thomas, from whose past a single incident is mentioned — seems to have had a childhood. Social and economic considerations have little to do with character in the world of *Q. E. D.* Everything turns back upon itself, nothing changes, and lives go nowhere. The deadlock we have seen dramatized throughout the tale finally receives explicit statement; and, once that happens, the author brings the story to an end. She has explored the possibilities inherent in her characters and has brought us back to where we started.

If Stein's work is either cyclic or non-progressive, then it is very much within the tradition of such Modernist fiction as Hemingway's *The Sun Also Rises* and Joyce's *Finnegans Wake*, two works similar in the cyclic nature of their "plots." For Stein, fictional "plot" does not have to go anywhere; and reader attention must be focused exclusively on the consciousness of the character and on the style of the narrative presentation. She is not yet ready to make the leap into stylistic subjectivity of "Melanctha," but *Q. E. D.*, like the final works of Henry James, takes the old structures of the novel as far as they are to go short of fragmentation.

One aspect of Stein's writing to which we become immediately sensitive is the kind of narrative consciousness that tells each of her tales. She never attempts to create a transparent narrator, in the manner of Joyce, who disappears into the fabric of the text. Rather, she creates a consciousness that is always distinctly present in one way or another, that intrudes with information, that takes definite attitudes toward the characters. In *Q. E. D.*, the narrator assumes a tone of superior familiarity with the reader — a tone which enables Stein to establish a certain distance from her characters and which gives her an ironic control over how the reader responds to them.

Stein treats matters of selectivity in the manner of a short-story writer who dwells exclusively on a single theme. She gives us no information in *Q. E. D.* that does not focus directly on the triangular love relationship. However, within the narrow limitations of her material, Stein seems to speak of *everything* that has to do with her subject. We are spared nothing — not the smallest argument, the most tedious lovers' quarrel, or the most trivial visit. Life for Stein "consists of all the tedious monotony of most everyday existences and of repetition not only of boring habit, but also of events whose character is dictated by the basic nature of the individual."[11] This repetition of quotidian events becomes increasingly complex within the context of the developing interpersonal relationships; and yet the relationships do not lead to resolution, for Stein does not seem to believe in the possibility of endings.

In addition, she does not follow James's classic advice for young writers. She "states" a great deal more than she "renders." In fact, she seems to have a penchant for the nondramatic presentation of story, action, and dialogue. Apart from setting scenes with shorthand description, Stein portrays little physical movement; and the seemingly interminable conversations even in this short, early work are repetitious and circular, although always thematically relevant. Her characters exist as highly verbal consciousnesses, but not as the kind that E. M. Forster would have called "rounded."[12]

Q. E. D. adumbrates almost all the traits that Stein later uses self-consciously, although in its own right it is a carefully structured work. If Stein had continued in this mode, she might well have become a clever novelist of manners. But, as we shall see, something happened between the end of *Q. E. D.* and the end of *Three Lives*, the first "characteristic" Stein work, and still her most widely read piece of fiction.

II   Three Lives

Settled in Montparnasse at 27, rue de Fleurus, Gertrude Stein and her brother Leo became quickly acquainted with the emerging Modernist art and inevitably with many painters who lived in the artists' quarter. During this time, Stein continued the quiet work in her notebooks; and, in the spring of 1905, she began her next book, *Three Lives*, on which she proceeded steadily until she completed it the following February.[13] During this time, the "fauves" were first exhibited at the Autumn Salon, and Stein posed for the now famous portrait by Picasso that hangs in New York's Metropolitan Museum. In *The Autobiography of Alice B. Toklas*, she claims to have begun *Three Lives* by attempting a translation of Gustave Flaubert's *Trois Contes* while sitting beneath Cézanne's portrait of his wife,[14] a painting she and Leo purchased in December 1904. A search among her papers at Yale uncovered no trace of the translation — and Stein rarely threw anything away. But there is certainly no question that

she was strongly influenced by both Cézanne and Flaubert: by the
former, because of his sense that reality consisted primarily of underlying geometric structures; by the latter, because of his almost
obsessive concern with the perfection of style and with discovering
the absolute word, *le mot juste*.[15] At any rate, the similarities of both
"The Good Anna" and "The Gentle Lena" with Flaubert's "Un
Coeur Simple" are quite striking.

Three Lives consists of three long stories — "Melanctha" is the
length of a short novel — each of which details the life of a servant
girl. Although "Melanctha" appears second among the three, it was
composed last and exhibits most strongly the stylistic breakthrough
that Stein created very quietly while her loquacious brother enter-
tained the guests at their apartment. The models for both "The
Good Anna" and "The Gentle Lena" were servant girls who worked
for Stein while she studied medicine at Johns Hopkins. They are
similar to Flaubert's Félicité, the central figure in "A Simple Heart,"
for they are both childish and are presented by a narrator who
employs a condescending "wise-child" tone in describing them. In
neither of the stories, as in Flaubert's, is the emphasis on plot,
narrative movement, or drama. As we might expect, Stein is
primarily interested in using her characters to exemplify personality
types and in developing a narrative technique that goes beyond the
traditional novelistic convention of a story that moves chronologically. Stein's device is to take moments of time and develop each
of them individually; and in accumulating these moments her story
establishes its reality.

The more stylized language in these tales conveys a strong sense of
authorial confidence. Attributes such as repetition and arbitrary psychological typing that seem accidental in *Q. E. D.* are now exploited
with greater calculation. The opening sentence of "The Gentle
Lena" reads: "Lena was patient, gentle, sweet and german [sic],"[16];
nothing in the rest of the story describes Lena's character more
acutely than this typological description. Mannered repetition
appears on the first page of "The Good Anna":

Anna managed the *whole little house* for Miss Mathilda. It was a *funny
little house*. . . . They were *funny little houses*, two stories high, with red
brick fronts and long white steps.
This *one little house* was always very full with Miss Mathilda, an under
servant, stray dogs and cats and Anna's voice that *scolded, managed,
grumbled* all day long. (11; my italics)

The stylized repetition in this passage of *house* with variations, which many readers will recognize as intrinsic to Hemingway's descriptive technique (see the opening paragraphs of "In Another Country"), is used by Stein in 1905, almost twenty years before she had met the young Hemingway. The second paragraph is a summing-up sentence. In this favorite device Stein sums up not only all the essential attributes of particular personalities (as in the sentence from "The Gentle Lena"), but also the contents of their days (as in the above sentence). This shorthand technique enables her to focus attention on things other than the trivia of day-to-day existence.

The varieties of repetition in *Three Lives* are quite numerous. In many paragraphs Stein employs a single word again and again; on page 240, for instance, she uses the word "brown" repeatedly to describe Lena. A word repeated often enough ceases to have merely a set of lexical meanings; it assumes an almost incantatory significance that forces its way into the reader's consciousness by the sheer weight of repeated usage. A few pages later Stein describes how Lena was sick during her ocean voyage. By the time she uses the words "sick" and "die" three or four times, we are indelibly impressed by the sense of Lena's discomfort, even though the distance forced on us by the narrative summation is such that it prevents a vivid *rendering* of Lena's particular discomfort.

This use of incantatory repetition helps to establish both Anna and Lena as primitively simple personalities who are fixed in their modes of life and who think and do everything within the context of inexorable circumstance. Anna, for instance, is conscious of the peculiar kind of "ugliness" proper to each social class. The narrator speaks of how the people who borrow money from Anna act "in the kindly fashion of the poor" (65). Anna knows her place and accepts it; she lords it over the young girls who work in her kitchen, and she is deferential to her employer, Miss Mathilda. In addition, Stein believes in both racial and national types. She speaks of how one turns out if one has "a german [sic] husband to obey." She talks of how the "irish nature" determines behavior. In "Melanctha," her characters consider that the amount of white blood has a direct effect on the personality of a black person.

At other times, simple personality types are not determined by racial, national, or social origins; they are simply an innate part of the person. By virtue of its quite definable existence, the type becomes almost the whole of the personality. For instance, "Mrs. Drehten was a mild, worn, unaggressive nature that never cared to influence or to lead" (69). Nothing more need be said about her. This kind of psychological primitivism leads in *The Making of Americans* to an elaborate cataloging of hundreds of different types and in *A Long Gay Book* to an abortive attempt to list all the possible varieties of human personality. When Stein finally discovered that she could not compile a complete catalog of all humanity, she abandoned the portrayal of people and turned in *Tender Buttons* to describing things.

The narrative structure of *Three Lives* is more casual than the tight geometric patterning of *Q. E. D.*, for both "The Good Anna" and "The Gentle Lena" are highly episodic. In fact, the structure of each tale develops almost totally through the simple accretion of episodes. Stein follows both characters over a long period of years, limiting her observations to a few representative aspects of their lives to give us the sense that she has described only the essential aspects of Anna and Lena. We see the former with Miss Mathilda, with her dogs, and with a few of her friends. We watch Lena with her employers, with Mrs. Haydon (her aunt and the one person who takes an interest in her), and with the Kreders, whose son Herman she marries. When the characters' stories are over, they die. Because Stein is now more comfortable with an episodic structure, she is able to fragment time whenever she wishes. The escape from chronological narrative continuity gets us ready for the leap she takes toward fragmentation in "Melanctha" and in *The Making of Americans*.

The narrative consciousness of *Three Lives* is used with great sophistication, for it is blended into the total voice of the book. "He not only reflects the dialect of the characters, but he expresses the inarticulate thoughts of the characters in the very language that they would use were they able to express their thoughts for themselves."[17] Stein continues to use her "wise-child" simplicity of diction and often inverts the syntax to give an effect of language being translated, in this example: "And so when any day one might need life and help from others of the working poor, there was no way a woman who had a little saved could say them no" (65). In addition, Stein's narrator is more than willing at any time to put in his two cents about any subject. He has obviously never heard about the rules against such intrusiveness.

III "*Melanctha*"

"Melanctha" is Stein's best known piece of fiction. Although long and sometimes maddeningly repetitious, it has been anthologized more than once. It is probably the first story by a white American to deal with black people as people, and not merely as an outgrowth of the minstrel show. Although the story's tone often strikes a modern reader as somewhat patronizing, "Melanctha" has had no stronger defender than the black novelist Richard Wright, who tells of having read it during the Depression to a group of black workers. Wright had been accused by his comrades in the Communist party of having decadent taste because he admired Gertrude Stein. But the overwhelmingly favorable response of the black workers to the story and especially to the rhythms of Stein's language made Wright cease to doubt his enthusiasm for "Melanctha."[18]

Melanctha Herbert, the title character, is a young, footloose woman entering adulthood. Her closest friend is a married woman named Rose Johnson who lives in Bridgeport, an eastern city obviously modeled on Baltimore. Stein makes much of Melanctha's racial heritage, although not much of her being a servant girl, and focuses most of the story on Melanctha's sexual awakening.

Melanctha falls in love with a young black doctor, Jefferson Campbell, who treats her mother during her final illness. We watch Melanctha lead on the slow-moving, middle-class Jeff during the long central section which is concerned at great length with the development of their relationship. It is, in fact, the inner working of that relationship, the unfolding psychological impact the characters have on one another with which Stein is most concerned. We are witness much more to their thoughts about one another than to the things they do together.

When, after many pages, the affair between Melanctha and Jeff Campbell ends, we see her take up with another man, Jem Richards — a footless ne'er-do-well himself — with whom she has an equally unsuccessful relationship, although for different reasons. At the end of the story, Melanctha becomes sick, goes to a home for consumptives, and dies. The conclusion occurs quickly and offhandedly, in much the same fashion as the endings occur in the other two tales.

Of the scope of "Melanctha," Donald Sutherland has said: "Where 'The Good Anna' and 'The Gentle Lena' are composed as the presentation of a single type in illustrative incidents, 'Melanctha' is composed on the dramatic trajectory of a passion. . . . The events considered in 'Melanctha' are mostly the movements of the passion, how Jeff and Melanctha feel differently toward each other from moment to moment."[19] Sutherland's observations are acute, for "Melanctha" is no longer concerned with merely presenting one psychological type in great detail; its focus has now increased to an interest in developing a complex relationship among two or more characters who represent different psychological types. Also, there is a "story" in "Melanctha," but its development as narrative is quite different from that of conventional fiction. Stein presents a love relationship and many of the tensions attendant upon it; she also creates a certain amount of suspense concerning the outcome of the affair; but, despite these concerns, the major focus of interest is not how the story will turn out. Instead, the emphasis is mainly on the relationship of Melanctha and Jeff within the isolated moments of the story rather than on the overall outcome of their personal problems.

The story begins in present time with the birth and death of Rose Johnson's baby, but we are back within a few pages in Melanctha's childhood. This switch in time is more than just a simple flashback, however; it is Stein's method of presenting the personality type to which Melanctha belongs. She establishes Melanctha's character by reference to the familial and racial characteristics she cannot escape. Melanctha's father was a "big black virile negro"; her mother, obviously lighter skinned, perhaps white, was "wandering and mysterious and uncertain." The emphasis on racial determinism is made quite apparent on the second page:

> Rose Johnson was careless and lazy, but she had been brought up by white folks and she needed decent comfort. Her white training had only made for habits, not for nature. Rose had the simple, promiscuous unmorality of the black people.
> Melanctha Herbert was a graceful, pale yellow, intelligent, attractive negress. She had not been raised like Rose by white folks but then she had been half made with real white blood. (86)

The tone of the narrator is ambiguous. The statement "she had been brought up by white folks and she needed decent comfort" is a close enough approximation of black speech to qualify as a narrative echo of the story's ethos. But the final sentence of the first paragraph seems clearly a statement that purports to be analytic yet is, despite its sentimental overtones, a patronizing judgment even though it is "true" within the context of the story.

And yet, Stein's attitudes toward blacks, though often as naive as many of her psychological assertions, are still of a piece with her overall view of human nature. Everything that people do in the world of mind and body, matter and air, time and space, is strictly secondary to what they are inside — to the generalized type to which they belong. As a result, Stein must define her characters by psychological category before she can actually set them loose to move among other people with a physical environment. This kind of deductive characterization, basic to all of Stein's work, begins with a vengeance in "Melanctha" in which setting almost totally disappears except for a few descriptive passages; in which characters become disembodied consciousnesses that move in an environment composed entirely of their interpersonal relationships. This conception of character is the major facet of Stein's early abstractionism — more even than her celebrated style which is itself an outgrowth of her conception of character. If Stein's style becomes characteristically repetitious, it is not simply that she decided to affect a stylistic eccentricity; it is that she sees all of life as composed of continuously repeated actions and reactions which her style of writing must reflect.

Another basic Stein concept, manifest for the first time, is that the only important sense of historical time is the present. Since all action does take place in a present moment and since each human being expresses his basic nature through repeated action, the only valid way to describe a character is to report the repetitions of his behavior during continuously present moments. This doctrine of the continuous present affects Stein's writing in a number of ways; first of all, in the structure of her narrative. In "Melanctha," Stein concentrates on individual moments of present time rather than on a continuous narrative line that flows steadily from past through present to future. As we have seen, Stein can switch quite easily from the present into a past moment — not because the past is either real or important in itself, but because each individual is a presently existent entity who embodies the sum of all he or she has done in each of the continuously present moments that comprise what we now call "the past." Because of this conception of time, even though Stein's narratives are in one sense episodic, they are in another sense highly unified because she concentrates in each separate moment upon the same set of qualities that defines the basic nature of her characters.

In addition, Stein develops a self-conscious use of the present participle, a stylistic facet about which most critics have commented. This grammatical form expresses the continuous present by its very existence. To say, for instance, that a man "was doing" something is not the same as saying that he "did" something, for in the very morphology of -*ing* we are told that, even though the action took place in past time, it was an action that occurred progressively, as all actions must. To make clear the extent to which Stein began to use the present participle, we can cite two strikingly similar passages from her first two books. If there is real substance to the suggestion that "Melanctha" is basically a reworking of *Q. E. D.*, these passages provide some support.[20] Early in the novella, Adele asks Helen, "Tell me how much do you care for me." Helen answers, "Care for you my dear, more than you know and less than you think" (65). In "Melanctha," Jeff Campbell asks, "Tell me just straight out how much do you care for me, Miss Melanctha." The response is, "I certainly do care for you Jeff Campbell less than you are always thinking and much more than you are knowing" (132). The replacement of "think" and "know" by their participial variants is indicative of the shift in Stein's writing, a shift that finds her stressing the continuous present by using a stylistic device that exemplifies it.

To demonstrate Stein's use of the present participle in yet another way, I shall quote a paragraph of descriptive narration from "Melanctha" in which I have italicized all the present participial forms:

Jeff Campbell then began again on the old papers. He sat there on the steps just above where Melanctha was *sitting*, and he went on with his *reading*, and his head went *moving* up and down, and sometimes he was *reading*, and sometimes he was *thinking* about all the things he wanted to be *doing*, and then he would rub the back of his dark hand over his mouth, and in between he would be *frowning* with his *thinking*, and sometimes he would be *rubbing* his head hard to help his *thinking*. And Melanctha just sat still and watched the lamp *burning*, and sometimes she turned it down a little, when the wind caught it and it would begin to get to *smoking*. (119)

This long reflective moment takes place when Dr. Jefferson Campbell comes to watch over the final illness of "Mis" Herbert, Melanctha's mother. The two lovers are having the first of many conversations during which they try to justify their respective life styles. Since each one represents to the other a polar concept of how to live, the relationship of Jeff and Melanctha is doomed to repeat itself fruitlessly again and again. The impasse they reach in this particular incident is reflected by Jeff's sitting and brooding as he attempts to respond in some way to Melanctha.

The difference made by the present participles is quite important; for this is not simply the relation of a past incident. The grammatical form that embodies the ongoing process gives us a sense of the con-

tinuous changes that take place in Jeff's consciousness from moment
to moment as he broods. This marriage of language and theme works
beautifully if the reader accepts the repetitive nature of Stein's concept of human personality. It is process *within* a moment rather than
process from moment to moment that is at the core of "Melanctha"'s structure, for the totality of the story consists of an accretion
of such moments within which the continuous present is exhibited in
the process of its development. The moment "is a 'still point' within
which there is movement."[21]

In "Melanctha," the narrative consciousness is a flexible voice
that sometimes stands back from the action to judge the characters;
at other times, it speaks from directly within their consciousness. The
narrator's speech-rhythms reflect almost completely the sensibility
that informs the dialogue. Syntax is often juggled to approximate the
so-called Negro dialect. Rather than take a metaphorical tape
recorder into the room with Jeff and Melanctha, Stein prefers to approximate their speech rhythms as evidence of their inner natures.
That no person in "real life" speaks in so extended and repetitious a
manner is obvious; but since all fictional dialogue is, to begin with,
arbitrarily selected by the author, why then must it mime "reality"?
Stein lets her characters talk in long, stylized, repetitious speeches to
present the reader with a symbolic sense of their innermost natures,
which we must infer from the evidence given us primarily in
dialogue. Stein chooses the generalized manner of Melanctha's
speech from the limited number of possibilities open within the
bounds of her basic nature.

Stein makes a concentrated use throughout "Melanctha" of motif
words and phrases. One phrase is "the wide abandoned laughter that
makes the warm broad glow of negro sunshine." She uses this in
relation to a number of the characters, stating that they either have
or do not have the quality. The repeated use of such a motif has the
function of suggesting a continuous quality present in the implied
ethnic environment as well as making it possible for the author to
show variations on that quality within the fixed nature of that environment. She can thus suggest both permanence and change.
Other motif words are "wandering" and "wisdom." They are intentionally undefined, but they are often euphemistic about sexual
knowledge and about the process of coming to such "wisdom." Occasionally, however, to heighten the impact of her euphemisms and
perhaps to keep the reader on the toes of his or her own consciousness, Stein uses one of these words conventionally.

At other times, for emphasis through simple repetition, Stein opens every sentence of a paragraph with the same words or names. There is an element of sheer playfulness here, but there is often something subtler at work. On page 165, for instance, the words "always" or "always now" appear in almost every sentence. This usage is a paradox, since "always" suggests something repeated and timeless and "now" suggests only the immediate present. But Stein's position is that, although human nature is fixed and repetitive, we can come to know the inner nature of a person only by watching how it manifests itself in the continuously present moment. The paradox of the phrase "always now" suggests this very view of the world.

Stein's conception of human personality is already monolithic in "Melanctha," and it becomes even more so later on. In speaking of certain kinds of fixed personality types, she discusses on page 186 the differences between "tender hearted natures" and "passionate natures." This prefigures the discussion of personality types that is the basic subject of *The Making of Americans*, but it also reminds us that Melanctha's character was fixed by her racial and genetic heritage; it gives us the unalterable sense that her life could never have been changed, no matter what. Depending on her sexual partner, Melanctha is either dominant or dominated. With Jeff Campbell, she wins; with Jem Richards, she loses. It is in this pairing of personalities that Stein is always interested — as we recall from *Q. E. D.*, and as we shall see in *The Making of Americans*.

The fixed nature of personality and the totally determined sense of human destiny constitutive to Stein's world-view is made artistically viable by the shift in *Three Lives* — especially in "Melanctha" — to an emphasis on structure and style as the central way to express meaning. The potential for sentimentality to which Stein was prey even in *Q. E. D.* is now handled with ironic detachment, and that sentimentality is increasingly excised from her writing. This new emphasis on structure and style is part of the essential pattern of the most innovative Modernist literature, for it enables the writer to switch the focus of violation away from the characters and on to the language and form of the work of art. Having found her essential stylistic focus in "Melanctha," Stein is now able to go through an almost bewildering succession of innovations; and yet, as she does so, she always maintains the same conceptions of human personality that she first displayed as an undergraduate in the psychology laboratory.

CHAPTER 3

The Making of Americans

The Making of Americans (1925), Gertrude Stein's most ambitious book, occupied her on and off from 1902 to 1911. It has not, however, been very widely read; for its 925 closely printed pages[1] have overcome even the best-intentioned readers. Edmund Wilson, who devoted an entire chapter to Stein in Axel's Castle, had this to say: "I confess that I have not read this book all through, and I do not know whether it is possible to do so."[2] Even in the abridged version[3] (416 more liberally spaced pages), the difficulties inherent in Stein's prose still remain. Now that both the long and short versions of The Making of Americans[4] are in print, the number of potential readers has been increased. Still, perhaps the best way for an uninitiated reader to approach The Making of Americans would be through the dramatized version ("An Opera and a Play"), recently adapted by Leon Katz.[5] Katz, who knows as much about the novel as anybody, has remained faithful to both the "story" and the spirit of the original. After an acquaintanceship with this short dramatic version, the reader will be much better prepared for the rigors of either the abridged or the full-length book.

Like most of Stein's works, The Making of Americans was written long before publication.[6] From the evidence contained in her notebooks, she began it even before Three Lives, perhaps as early as 1902. In his unpublished doctoral dissertation, Leon Katz[7] has made a detailed study of the composition, intellectual background, and thematic structures of The Making of Americans. From his study of the voluminous notebooks that Stein kept from 1902 to 1911, Katz has been able to piece together the continuous development of Stein's compositional ideas as well as the ways in which she used characters and incidents from her own life. On the rebound from the unhappy love affair on which she based Q. E. D., Stein busied herself with reading English prose narrative at the British Museum.

Her notebooks detail this reading as well as her personal relationships during the early years of the century. It was a time of loneliness and despair, and the picture that emerges from these notebooks is quite at variance with the ebullient, arrogant, and totally controlled Gertrude Stein of *The Autobiography of Alice B. Toklas.* (The notebooks, under Katz's editorship, have been announced for publication by Liveright.)

There are also five chapters remaining of an early draft of the novel that were finally published as "The Making of Americans" in 1971.[8] These chapters, composed sometime during 1903, were the first she wrote; and they show that Stein had started her major work years before sitting down to write the final draft in 1908. In fact, along with "Fernhurst,"[9] these 1903 chapters antedate both *Q. E. D.* and *Three Lives;* and they are fascinating indices of the basic materials with which Stein was always to work.

From the start, she was concerned with such matters as the "tempers" of individual characters, the relationship between the "inside" and the "outside" of a person, and "the opposition in resemblance" (147) of two or more characters. Leon Katz maintains that "the original plan of the novel concerned a single family [the Dehnings], not two as in the final version."[10] "The Making of Americans" bears out this contention since its emphasis is on the Dehning family, particularly on Julia; the Herslands, who are the major focus of the completed novel, are there only peripherally, and only because it is Henry Hersland to whom Julia gets married.

The original concept of the novel seems to have been that of a conventional family chronicle, perhaps like *Buddenbrooks* which Thomas Mann had published a few years before. In Stein's earlier drafts, particularly in "Fernhurst," she shows a sharp eye for manners and detail, an ideal attribute for social fiction, and a quality we have already observed in *Q. E. D.* But her concept of character ultimately controls her achievement. Mann, for instance, is at his best in *Buddenbrooks* in creating a specific sense of environment; and his characters move in a rendered world of material entities and detailed interpersonal relationships. Stein's conception of character, however, is much more abstract; and she is not very interested finally in environmental details. Even in these early drafts, she makes absolute statements about psychological types; and she is more concerned with the truth of her abstractions than with rendering her characters "realistically." Indeed, the writing of "Melanctha" transmuted the shape of *The Making of Americans*

from its original project into a panorama of psychological types who
are paraded slowly before the reader in a langorous, mannered, and
repetitious style. Plot and physical detail eventually play almost no
part in the narrative.

I *The "Plot" of* The Making of Americans

Since the plot plays such a little role, it is difficult to give a
coherent summary of the story of *The Making of Americans.* The
"plot," such as it is (it is difficult to give up the word), does not
develop; it meanders. But, since its meandering follows the mean-
derings of the author's mind as she meditates on her subject, the
erratic course of this mammoth book is not without its ultimate
direction. Stein's basic intentions are suggested by her title: she is interested in analyzing the process by which "Americans" develop out
of generations of immigrants. But her focus is no more sociological
than it was scientific when she worked in the Harvard psychology
laboratory. She is interested in writing about her own family and
personal background: and, to give these matters more importance,
she attempts to generalize about the American character from them.
The novel is constructed around five "books," four long ones —
broken into sections — and a short concluding coda.

The first book introduces the novel's two central families, the
Herslands and the Dehnings. The Herslands originate from Gertrude Stein's family, for the older David Hersland is based on her
father; Alfred, on her brother Michael; and Martha, on herself. The
Herslands eventually settle in Gossols (Oakland), and the Dehnings
settle in Bridgepoint (Baltimore). One complicating factor in *The
Making of Americans* is that there are often a number of characters
with the same names (there are three or four Davids and Marthas,
for instance), a habit that stems not from Stein's carelessness but
from her desire to show that the immigrant generations of Americans
are basically inhabited by individuals who are similar in character.

While there is a minimal amount of story in Book 1, Stein rapidly
loses interest in actual events and begins to meditate on the "bottom
natures" of her characters and of their experience. One of the first
things to disappear from the fabric of her fiction is dialogue, a staple
of "Melanctha." As Stein meditates on the nature and typology of
human character, her sentences begin to grow longer and more complex, a fact well documented by Richard Bridgman.[11] The sentences
are increasingly analytical and minutely detailed in their quite simple variations, and they become schematized into repeated and

recognizable patterns, a phenomenon I shall discuss later; the resulting diction exhibits a vocabulary full of simple code words and phrases. The final section of Book 1 demonstrates this process quite strongly because Stein devotes herself in it to a discussion of the various types of human personality. On many occasions, she introduces what in any other novel would simply be extraneous minor characters; we wade through an unsteady progression of friends, seamstresses, and governesses, many of whom are dropped and never picked up again. Richard Bridgman suggests that, by the end of the last part of Book 1, Stein had established her habit of giving more attention to description than to narration, and of attempting the most simplistic kinds of explanation and understanding. "And on top of it all, she was purging her psyche of old ghosts."[12] Book 1 ends on page 285.

Book 2 is subtitled "Martha Hersland" and runs for almost two hundred pages. Since Martha was the character Stein modeled on herself, this section is heavily autobiographical. It begins with a long, tedious section that details in ritualized schematic sentences Stein's theories about how to recognize the "bottom nature of someone." In this book she explores the bottom nature of her own thinly veiled persona. We learn of Martha's childhood, her relationship with her father, her abortive sexual adventures with a boy from the block, her feelings about a governess named Madeleine Wyman, and her experiences at college. Stein has Martha marry Phillip Redfern, a character based on Leon Solomons, Stein's collaborator on one of her articles in the *Psychological Review*. Stein's instincts failed her here, however; she had earlier written an episode[13] based on the unfortunate marriage of a man named Alfred Hodder to a Bryn Mawr professor. She tried to combine Solomons and the philandering Hodder into Redfern, but the fusion did not result in a coherent character. As a result, the portrait of Martha Hersland is not fully realized either, perhaps also because its emotional focus is so mixed up with Stein's own search for identity.

The third book of *The Making of Americans* is entitled "Alfred and Julia Hersland," and it is even longer than the second. Ironically, however, this book has very little to say specifically about its two characters. Stein has become even more impatient with her novel's structure, and she gives herself increasingly to abstract ruminations. The narrative consciousness of *The Making of Americans* has taken over almost completely; and it diminishes story line, physical detail, and simple events to nothing. Subject matter is now exclusively the author's consciousness ruminating on its present contents. Quite naturally, such a consciousness has no patience with characters who, the longer the author writes about them, become creatures of the distant past.

In Book 4, "David Hersland," this process with the author's consciousness has taken over completely; and whatever remains of Stein's previously held novelistic conventions disappears. This section, which ostensibly is about David Hersland's life and death, gives way completely to the narrator's meditations and to Stein's present, real-life distractions. No other characters even receive names in this part of the book. Bridgman has suggested that the younger David Hersland is based on Stein's brother Leo and that the death of David at the end of this book is Stein's symbolic way of freeing herself from Leo's domination.[14] It is fitting that Leo Stein left the rue de Fleurus household in 1913, soon after the end of the composition of *The Making of Americans;* for his centrality in Gertrude's affections had long been lost to Alice Toklas. Whether or not Bridgman is right, Stein was obviously obsessed with the subject of death; and this section of *The Making of Americans* is full of her meditations about it.

By this time, Stein is clearly exhausted with the labor of her book and also quite bored by it. Its nearly half a million words and its endless series of tortured sentences have taught her not only what it means to write a novel but also that she can never again sustain anything like a long piece of conventional narrative prose. By the end of the novel, she is plunged fully into what we now think of as her characteristic abstractionism. The final book, "History of a Family's Progress," is a short coda of only twenty pages; it is without characters; and it exists wholly within the narrator's ruminative consciousness. The scope of the book, which had begun on such a grand scale, has now narrowed almost to the vanishing point of solipsism.

II *The Implications of* The Making of Americans

To read *The Making of Americans* at all, we have to suspend most of the expectations we bring to reading a novel and surrender ourselves completely to the author. We have to become captives of Stein's rhythms, of her insights into generalized human character, and of the slow, almost torturous unfolding of the "story." We must accept a narrative tone that is even more simplistic and "primitive" than in "Melanctha." And we have to forget completely about drama, for this novel is the first full-length one to escape almost totally from the convention that narrative fiction must contain a story. If *The Making of Americans* had not had to wait until 1925 to be published, the course of modern fiction might very well have been different.

Can we then legitimately call this a novel? Although the most interesting Modernist works invariably blur generic lines, I think it important that we try to define the genre Stein was evolving. George Knox has suggested that *The Making of Americans* may be Stein's parodistic version of the Great American Novel,[15] for the very nature of its scope and of its intention is to present a fictional construct of how the American character developed. In the largest cultural sense, Knox is correct; but his assumption comprehends only subject matter and scope. It does not help us define Stein's form beyond calling it parodistic; and even that use of the word is somewhat special, since it is obvious that Stein was deadly serious about most of the book.

The subtitle is "The History of a Family's Progress," but is it useful to call *The Making of Americans* a history? (For a while the working title of *Three Lives* was "Three Histories.") If history can be defined as a reporting of how past events unfolded chronologically in space and time, then this book certainly stretches the definition. And yet, Stein has many of the historian's attitudes. In addition to recapitulating events that occur in space and time, the historian is concerned with establishing a rationale for why these events happened. As a result, he is a theoretician of causes and outcomes. This analytic attitude toward people and events is basic to Stein's writing, and her subtitle directs our attention that way. She is an interpretive historian of the development of American personality types, albeit a historian with a weak sense of documentation, just as she is a novelist without the realists' concern for detail. Stein is much less interested in exemplification than in analysis. That she does not care to present information in the usual temporal order is something else that distinguishes her from the conventional historian and novelist, but I know of no laws that force historians to follow a linear progression in time.

Stein makes a number of statements that express her historical self-consciousness:

Sometime there is a history of each one. There must be such a history of each one for the repeating in them makes a history of them. The repeating of the kinds of them makes a history of the kinds of them, the repeating of the different parts and ways of being makes a history in many ways of every one. This is now a history of some. This will be sometime a history of many kinds of them. Any one who looks at each one will see coming out from them the bottom nature of them and the mixing of other nature or natures with the bottom nature of them.[16]

Not, obviously, a historian of political, economic, or cultural events, Stein is the historian of different kinds of personality types; her documentary evidence consists of the actions of fictional individuals who repeat continuously their essential "bottom natures." She treats her characters with the detachment of a social scientist: "Sometime there will be a complete history of Madeleine Wyman's married living, it will be very interesting" (265). How far we wish to go with this metaphor is not so important as our realization of how difficult it is to define a genre for the classification of this mammoth book.

In stretching narrative structures, Stein uses a number of devices; and each is designed to make her book more abstract. For one thing, she excises all movement. She has gone so far away from the Jamesian dictum to "render" that she is now involved almost totally in statement and analysis. Congruent with her new method of telling is the self-conscious use of various forms of repetition, some of which I shall discuss in detail. The functional value of her repetitions, however, is quite clear when we understand that the major intention behind the pseudo-historical narrative of *The Making of Americans* is the author's desire to capture in some way "the slow, evergoing passage of time from moment to moment and from generation to generation."[17] In addition, Stein begins what is to become a progressive evolution in her writing: the excision from her language of most of the traditional rewards of a variable literary style. She eschews as much as possible — and especially as the book continues — imagery, metaphor, paradox, and most of the well-known devices of figurative language. These linguistic forms are not completely absent, but their appearance is rare enough to draw our attention.

She also continues her tendency to disorient and distort standard English syntax. She is a primitivist in that she completes statements normally "understood" by adding the words left out, much as a child might do. She uses participles as substantives. Aside from being thematically functional, these devices draw attention to themselves and make the reader conscious at all times that this work is being *written*. Language for Stein is more than just a transparent vehicle of sense. By drawing attention to the very materials of her narrative —

particularly its words — Stein creates a work that has an ontological autonomy that most Modernist artists spent their lives struggling to create. Aside from its sheer bulk, *The Making of Americans* exists very solidly in its own universe. Its contingency upon the "real" world is minimal, and Stein will reduce such contingency even more in later works.

As I have already suggested, the function of the narrator is essential to this book. In *Q. E. D.* and *Three Lives*, Stein maintained the pretense of at least some distinction between the author and the narrative consciousness, but in *The Making of Americans* this pretense breaks down. The words are definitely being written by a consciousness named Gertrude Stein who makes her presence felt at all times and who, whenever she feels like it, simply leaps into the narrative. She is at once a scientist who must always explain both her conclusions and how she reaches them,[18] and a fabulist who begins her book with a short parable told in the tone of a fairy tale: "Once an angry man dragged his father along the ground through his own orchard. 'Stop!' cried the groaning old man at last, 'Stop! I did not drag my father beyond this tree' " (3).

The fabulist tone makes even more tenable the almost total lack of temporal specificity, for fables take place outside of time; and, if the experience of all generations of immigrants to the United States is the same, then it does not matter which time we refer to when we discuss particular individuals. By its very nature, The Great American Novel must create a myth of the American character, a fable that expresses the "bottom nature" of the American experience, a parable that is true for all ages and places; and such fiction has, therefore, no obligation to be specific about either time or place. Accordingly, we have no notion of what the houses looked like in which the Herslands and the Dehnings lived, and we do not know exactly where Gossols and Bridgepoint are. But we do know what general classes of people live in particular sections of each of these geographically unlocated towns. Social classes are, as we have seen, important to Stein's abstract sense of human character; and they are, as such, much more important than any detailed descriptions.

As for temporal continuity, Stein fractures it even more than she did in "Melanctha." She mentions events early in the book that she drops for five hundred or six hundred pages, and she refers to them later with the assumption that we have remembered them the whole time. Joyce, after all, makes similar demands in *Ulysses;* but, since a work of art for both writers is an autonomous unit with a highly integrated texture and structure, all parts of it are equally important; and all must play a continuously integral part in the development and, indeed, in the very existence of the book. We cannot be expected to know anything about these novels unless we know everything about them. And, since the physical book has a continuously present existence, so does the narrative contained within its covers. Therefore, we have the sense, in reading both Stein and Joyce, that future and past are only names for relationships with the present moment, the only moment that has any real existence. For Joyce the present is very specific and heavily textured; for Stein it is more abstract and historical; for both, the present is all that there is.

Since Stein stretches her narrative so much, it is incumbent upon the reader to put the "story" together for himself. In this sense, *The Making of Americans* has the same intention as the paintings of Matisse and Picasso, two of Stein's close friends at that time. Both painters obligated the viewer to participate actively in perceiving the work of art in its all-at-onceness and in working out the parameters of its configuration for himself. Matisse and Picasso each wished to recapture the mentality of the child whose perceptual apparatus is not yet fully conditioned. The distortions of perspective and linear continuity that we see in their works are symbolic assertions that perceptual "unity" is a cultural convention and that the artist who realizes this is free to create his or her own configurations. The perceiver's obligation is to accept such configurations by involving himself actively in the process of perceptually completing the painting's form.

Stein accepts these new conventions in all her work, but in *The Making of Americans* she first breaks through into the genuinely Modernist vision which demands that we grasp a work of art in its totality before we can come to terms with any part of it. If this is an unreasonable assumption about the limits of human attention, we must nonetheless take it into account before judging the success or failure of *The Making of Americans*. Because the reader must now fit together for himself all the pieces of the puzzle, Stein feels less and less obligation to continuous narrative. As a result, the book becomes an increasing tapesty of digressions, so much so that at times the digressions are the book's main focus. But the real subject matter of *The Making of Americans* is the contents of Stein's consciousness. She stops the narrative occasionally to tell us of some things she would like to do: "I want to know sometime all about sentimental feeling" (480). At other times she talks about the books she will write next: "Sometime then I will give a history of all of them and that will be a long book and when I am finished with this one and then I will begin that one" (479). She refers here to *A Long Gay Book*, which she began to write concurrently with *The Making of Americans* and which she dropped a year later. Stein even gives vent to momentary frustrations: "I am all unhappy in this writing" (348).

For Stein, in contrast to T. S. Eliot, art does not extinguish the author's personality;[19] indeed, her art celebrates it. Although the book is an autonomous object, it can achieve its autonomy only by evolving in direct and open relationship with the author who creates it and who always remains part of it. Stein uses no authorial or illusionist tricks; she is always publicly pulling the strings and directing the traffic. It is almost as though the struggle of a work of art to exist is a sufficient embodiment of its form. If Stein decides to omit those parts of her personality she no longer wants to display, that too is her privilege because, in all her works from now on, she reigns like a not-quite-benevolent monarch.

As a monarch, Stein is capricious about which fictional techniques she wishes to retain and which she promises to keep. She withholds information constantly. She tells us the name of only one governess of the Hersland children, Madeleine Wyman. She intimates early in the book that Alfred Hersland is a dishonest man, but she never tells us what he does that is dishonest. The specific fact of Alfred Hersland's dishonesty is part of the "buried narrative" that Leon Katz has reconstructed;[20] but, as far as the finished product is concerned, Stein feels no need to tell us any more of the story than she desires. There are occasions when she makes the reader wait interminably for the fulfillment of a promise. At one point, she says, "This is now a history of Martha Hersland. This now a history of Martha and of everyone who came to be of her living" (290); but we wait one hundred pages before the author actually begins the story she has promised; she has spent the intervening time digressing on personality types.

But, at times, she does the reverse and tells us how a situation will turn out even before she gets us started on the story proper. As soon as she marries Alfred Hersland to Julia Dehning, Stein tells us immediately that "They were not successful together in their married living" (602); but she does not tell us why. Having presented the reader with her two characters and having analyzed their personality types, Stein feels that she has done enough, that the reader can figure out the determined necessity by which the marriage had to

fail. Her procedure is certainly a reversal of the usual convention;
but that is her intent; for the Modernist artist is bound to no conventions other than those that the work of art creates for itself.

Stein's use of repetition is the most striking carry-over from
"Melanctha." Most writers go out of their way *not* to repeat, at least
not to do so noticeably; but Stein parades her repetitions with
arrogance. In fact, the varieties of repetition in *The Making of
Americans* are so numerous that it would be tedious to list them all.
However, the discussion of a few of them shows how they exemplify
Stein's view of the way basic human nature exists in a continuous
present. In one of her *Lectures in America*, "The Gradual Making of
The Making of Americans," Stein says:

> I then began again to think about the bottom nature in people, I began to
> get enormously interested in hearing how everybody said the same thing
> over and over again with infinite variations but over and over again until
> finally if you listened with great intensity you could hear it rise and fall and
> tell all that that there was inside them, not so much by the actual words they
> said or the thoughts they had but the movement of their thoughts and words
> endlessly the same and endlessly different.[21]

This rationale was stated many years after the fact; but, in examining her unpublished notebooks, Leon Katz has shown that Stein had
the same explicit concerns when she was composing *The Making of
Americans*.[22]

Aside from Stein's using phrasal *leitmotifs* such as "the ten acre
place in the part of Gossols where no other rich people were living,"
she makes repeated redefinitions of the nature of her book, and she
usually begins them with something like, "This then is a history
of. . . ." She is always "beginning again," usually after one of her
many digressions, with "as I was saying," which is a sign to the
reader that she is now returning to her basic subject. Even more
striking is her continuous use of syntactic repetition, usually by having the same words appear in the same part of any number of consecutive sentences as in this representative example:

> I am thinking now about one kind and I am knowing now not really know-
> ing all of them but really knowing being in them in some of this kind in men
> and women. I am knowing three of them of this group of them as men. I am
> knowing one of a group of them as a woman. I am knowing another of
> another group in men and women as a woman, some of another group of

them some as men and some as women. I am knowing another very large group of them and I am knowing these as everything they ever are in living some of them. I am trying to begin now telling what I am knowing about sense in men and in women. (674)

It is important to notice how certain key words and phrases are used again and again, usually in the same place in consecutive sentences, and always with a slight variation, so that the accumulated effect is not simply the repetitive beat of a tom-tom but a sense of multiplicity within arbitrary limitations. Stein feels that all human beings live within such limitations because the "bottom natures" into which they are born and within which they are reared are unchangeable. Still, within the limits of an unchanging and repetitive "bottom nature," individuals can show subtle variations.

Stylistically, Stein anticipates the full-scale development of a new form which she will define in her "portraits" and which I call the "cinema technique." She proceeds, as in a moving picture, to repeat almost exactly the same image in each frame; but, in the cinema, each frame has a subtle variation so that, when the film is passed quickly through the projector, the viewer perceives on the screen the sensation of movement. And such is the intent of Stein's "cinema technique." If we could read her writing with the same speed as the spin of the projector, we could get a similar sensation of movement. After *The Making of Americans* the movement in Stein's fictional prose depends on such subtle repetitions and variations.

Stein wishes to explore more than just the "bottom natures" of individual personalities. Her deepest intention, as it was in "Melanctha," is to show how different personality types relate to one another. She presents these relationships in two main areas in *The Making of Americans:* the conflict between generations that she states in the opening lines of the book, and the interactions between the sexes.[23] The problem is that the more she abstracts her narrative from anything but an analytic context, the less she is able to show how convincing relationships can develop among various personality types. She is reduced too often simply to telling us what a relationship was like; and, as a result, *The Making of Americans* becomes more an abstract catalog of individual personality types than a compendium of relationships among human beings. All the characters become grist for Stein's psychological mill; in fact, hierarchical distinctions begin to disintegrate because psychology is more important to the author than social class. *The Making of Americans* is one of the last attempts by a major author to reduce all of humanity to the working principles of a few psychological types.

The major grammatical form in the novel is the present participle, as we might expect, since *The Making of Americans* is so centrally concerned with the continuous present. Because Stein combines this form with the expansiveness of the "cinema technique," she needs more space. As a result, in this work the paragraph is the most important unit in her prose. Donald Sutherland has said of *The Making of Americans* that "each paragraph is made to be a complete interior event."[24] Individual sentences begin to depend more and more on their relationships to one another for their interest, movement, and meaning. Quite often the paragraphs seem arbitrarily juxtaposed, forcing the reader to discover for himself the transitional logic that is always there. Anyone accustomed to Modernist writing, however, should have no trouble getting used to such juxtapositions.

In the final pages of the book, Stein begins to experiment with new styles. She was obviously tiring of *The Making of Americans* after working on it for so many years, and she had already begun to write her "portraits." We begin to see passages that are not semantically continuous, as well as ones full of the kind of linguistic playfulness we associate with the portraits, the poetry, and the drama that Stein began to write very soon thereafter. For instance, here is an example of the semantically discontinuous, playful prose we shall see increasingly from now on: "He was sometimes then with more than ten. He was sometimes then with more than one. He was sometimes then with three. He was sometimes then with one. He was sometimes then with not any one. He was sometimes then with another one" (855).

The prose seems on the verge of discarding meaning and of beginning to treat words as plastic counters that can be moved at the will of the user. And this is precisely what Stein was to do as soon as she finished — no doubt with a sigh of relief — her version of the Great American Novel. Never again was she to try anything so ambitious. Having done it once, there was, after all, no need to do it again. Besides, in the process of composing *The Making of Americans*, she had discovered a host of new literary problems to solve. Her experiments in writing had just begun.

CHAPTER 4

The Portraits and Modernism

E VEN as Gertrude Stein brought *The Making of Americans*
to a close, she had already begun to develop other literary styles
and forms. We recall her ambition to write "a complete history of
every one who ever was or is or will be living."[1] This "history" was *A
Long Gay Book* on which she worked sporadically until 1912. During
four remarkably productive years, 1908 - 1912, she also wrote a
number of other works including "Portrait of Mabel Dodge at the
Villa Curonia," *Matisse Picasso and Gertrude Stein, Two: Gertrude
Stein and Her Brother*, and *Jenny, Helen, Hannah, Paul and Peter*.
In addition, she claimed she had developed a new literary form
which she called the "portrait."

Actually, this claim deserves some qualification. The "portrait" as
a literary form was in vogue in France in the late seventeenth century, particularly at the salons of Madeleine de Scudéry and Mlle. de
Montpensier, "La Grande Mademoiselle." As used then, it was a
verbal description of a person, often a self-portrait, and primarily a
vehicle for flattery or satire.[2] Stein was probably not familiar with
this form and developed her own version of the "portrait" out of her
contact with Modernist painting rather than by trying to resurrect an
archaic literary tradition.

At any rate, she tells how, sometime during 1908, she wrote
"Ada," a word portrait of Alice Toklas. With this experiment Stein
began what turned out to be the most extended flirtation of a writer
in English with the conventions of another artistic medium. To come
to terms with her work not only during this period but during the
rest of her life, we shall have to deal in some way with how Stein
adapted the conventions of painting to the medium of writing. The
capstone of this effort to create abstract word-paintings is *Tender
Buttons*, a series of still lifes completed in 1913. We shall focus
briefly on *A Long Gay Book* and *Two* before discussing the portraits

and still lifes because each of these longer works explores the styles that Stein was to develop more fully in the shorter ones.

I   A Long Gay Book

Years later, during her triumphant lecture tour of the United States, Stein recalled her ambition in writing *A Long Gay Book:* "As I say I began A Long Gay Book and it was to be even longer than The Making of Americans and it was to describe not only every possible kind of a human being, but every possible threes and fours and fives of human beings and every possible kind of crowds of human beings."[3] That she found this ambition impossible we have already seen, but the reader would never know from reading *A Long Gay Book* that it was unfinished. It contains no story at all, not even the "buried narrative" of *The Making of Americans.* For three-quarters of its length, it contains only a long list of psychological types and their characteristics, to which names are attached. Occasionally two names are mentioned together, from which we are to assume that a personal relationship is being developed. But to an even greater extent than its massive predecessor, *A Long Gay Book* renders neither action nor social setting, neither speeches nor physical settings. A textbook on psychological typology, it is made unusual because of the idiosyncratic way the author uses the English language; and it is certainly not a novel, not at least in any way that genre has been used before. A *Long Gay Book* breaks with tradition even more than did *The Making of Americans.*

In addition to its formal idiosyncrasies, *A Long Gay Book* is distinguished by the way it breaks at the end into what we now regard as the distinctive Stein style — a style characterized primarily by the nonmimetic, playful, and plastic use of words. Stein may have developed such a style because she became progressively more tired of trying the impossible in *A Long Gay Book* and decided to shift the grounds of her considerable talent for concentration to the language itself. Whatever the reasons, the book has changed completely by its end, and the only way we can tell that two distinctly different passages are from the same book is that both appear between the same covers.

Early in *A Long Gay Book*, this stylistic shift is not apparent. Stein states her basic subject matter almost immediately, demonstrating at this point a thematic continuity between the present book and its predecessor:

Every one has in them a fundamental nature to them with a kind of way of thinking that goes with this nature in them in all the many millions made of that kind of them. Every one then has it in them to be one of the many kinds of men or many kinds of women. There are many kinds of men and many kinds of women and of each kind of them there are always many millions in the world and any one can know by watching the many kinds there are of them and this is to be a history of all the kinds of them.[4]

Aside from the change of "bottom nature" to "fundamental nature," this style is still the same familiar one. As in *The Making of Americans*, Stein bases her characters on people she knew, except that she now uses their real names. Stein seems to have begun *A Long Gay Book* without fully realizing where it was going to go; and, since the published text is basically an unrevised first draft, the book as we now have it is not fictionalized to nearly the same extent that *The Making of Americans* was. Stein obviously felt that she no longer had even to "make up" a novel. She also continues — and to a much greater extent — to give herself directions and to explain everything about her creative process to the reader. As a result, the book's increasing emphasis is on the present moment of creation, and the narrative flow of traditional fiction is totally nonexistent. Stein attaches names to typological descriptions that in no way either render or describe them, and so there are, in essence, no "fictional" characters in *A Long Gay Book*. There are only names.

What is most immediately striking about this work is its increasing emphasis on word play. In the following sentences, traditional sense is much less important than the rhythmic use of internal rhyme and the ritualistic repetition of phrases: "Each day is every day, that is to say, any day is that day. Any day is that day that is to say if any day has been a day there will be another day and that day will be that day" (36). Stein is attempting to explore the essence of the simplest kinds of semantic units; and, although she makes us wait for her circular concepts to unfold, she nonetheless presents us with a thoroughly logical statement — and the logic is available to any reader with the patience to figure it out.

As the book proceeds, its paragraphs become shorter and shorter, and Stein begins to experiment with sentences that both cease to make conventional sense and yet still maintain traditional forms of semantic continuity. For instance: "A tiny violent noise is a yellow happy thing. A yellow happy thing is a gentle little tinkle that goes in all the way it has everything to say. It is not what there was when

it was not where it is. It is all that it is when it is all that there is" (82).
This kind of disorientational writing prefigures both *Tender Buttons* and the most experimental portraits. We do, after all, expect
sentences to make sense, especially when they follow standard grammar and syntax. The latter is basic to English sense; and, although
Stein does maintain traditional syntax, her words connect associa-
tionally but not logically as the form of the sentence leads us to expect. Nor do succeeding sentences in the same paragraph solve the
mystery; and it is obvious they are not intended to do so. For Stein,
language is a material to be shaped; and, if the artist wishes to dis-
pense with traditional structure and meaning, then we must look
elsewhere for what to extract from his words. Stein has heretofore
conditioned us to doing without plot, narrative continuity, drama,
and character; now we must give up meaning. No other writer had
ever had such *hubris*.

Freed now from most burdens that have encumbered writers in
English, Stein develops a use of language determined almost exclusively by association — both syntactical and intuitive — and
sound. For instance: "Pale pet, red pet, pink pet, blue pet, white pet,
dark pet, real pet, fresh pet, all the tingling is the weeding, the close
pressing is the tasting" (97). This complete paragraph from late in *A
Long Gay Book* demonstrates just how far Stein has moved from her
originally stated intentions. She is no longer concerned with writing
a history of "every possible kind of human being" (3). She is now im-
mersed totally in a world of words, one in which sounds and letters
are the living reality that can be created only by her consciousness.[5]

Like a child stimulated to repeating and punning by the associations of sounds, Stein is only minimally concerned with traditional
linguistic sense. She is interested primarily in expressing a kind of
verbal joy. It is as if she had just discovered that she can play with
words: "Notes. Notes change hay, change hey day. Notes change a
least apt apple, apt hill, all hill, a screen table, sofa, sophia" (115).

The book ends with a prose poem full of logical *non sequiturs* and
word play:

> Frank, frank quay.
> Set of keys was, was
> Lead kind in soap, lead kind in soap sew up. Lead
> kind in so up. Lead kind in so up.
> Leaves a mass, so mean. No shows. Leaves a mass
> cool will. Leaves a mass puddle.
> Etching. Etching a chief, none plush. (116)

Our job as critics is to follow the associations, puns, and rhymes, and our task as readers is to sit back and enjoy the linguistic virtuosity that we have watched develop yet another new style within the unfolding of *A Long Gay Book*. If adult readers think it easy to write in a semantically "meaningless" style for more than a few sentences, I urge them to try. At the same time, they might also try to paint "nonrepresentationally." Whether or not such attempts are worth making is another matter; but we should never dismiss such achievements as mere child's play. Child's play is easy only for a child. The Modernist primitives — by which I mean writers like Stein and painters like Picasso and Matisse — wish to rediscover the simpler joys and the perceptions of an earlier and more innocent time in their lives.[6] To accept their work in any way, we must at least understand the premises on which they base their art.

II   Two: Gertrude Stein and Her Brother

Two: Gertrude Stein and Her Brother, written around the same time (1910 - 1912), exemplifies another major style. Unlike *A Long Gay Book*, it is a narrative in much the same mode as *The Making of Americans*. It tells a definite story about Stein and her brother Leo and about the coming of Alice Toklas — a story much like the "buried narrative" of *The Making of Americans*, since the reader must have at least some outside information in order to understand the pattern of events. Although no characters are given their "real" names, we have a genuine sense of their fictional presence in a way we never have in *A Long Gay Book* no matter how many names are used. There is neither physical nor social setting in *Two*, and yet the continuous rhythmic presentation of character through repetition finally gives the reader a sense that the story is about solid personalities — ones deeply felt by the author — who live in "real" time and space.

Stein's term for the core of personality in *Two* is the individual's "sound," which is synonymous with "bottom" and "fundamental" natures. She mentions this "sound" in the first paragraph of the book and then repeats the word in every paragraph from there until page 64. This obsessively repetitive quality adds to the book's rhythmic development and to its sense of stylistic and narrative unity, but the biographical reason for the use of "sound" is almost certainly related to Leo Stein's growing deafness. Stein alternates passages about each of her characters so as to suggest interpersonal relationships much more successfully than she did in either *The*

Making of Americans or *A Long Gay Book*. And the strong emotions
that well up from the narrative consciousness can be attributed to
the fact that Stein wrote the book after Alice Toklas had moved into
the Stein apartment and had turned what had once been a cozy
relationship of dominant brother and apparently docile sister into an
uncomfortable *ménage à trois*. Leo was to leave the household
forever around 1913. Soon thereafter the siblings divided their paintings, and, as far as I can determine, they never spoke to each other
again.

Stein begins *Two* by displaying the similarities and contrasts she
felt at work in the relationship:

> They are very much alike. They both have sounds coming out of them.
> They are alike. They both of them have sounds coming out of them that
> have too much meaning for the ending that is sounding out from them.
> They are alike. They both of them are not knowing the beginning and end-
> ing in sound coming out of them. They are alike. They certainly are very
> much alike.
> They certainly are not at all alike. One of them is hearing himself and is
> having then sound come out of him. One of them is hearing some one and is
> then having sound come out of her.[7]

This passage embodies what I earlier called the "cinema technique."
In *The Making of Americans,* as we noted, paragraphs of interweav-
ing repetitions were often juxtaposed against other paragraphs
written in the same style but concerned with different subject
matter. In *Two*, there is a much tighter connection between
paragraphs, a connection established in the beginning by the obvious device of continuously using the word "sounds," and maintained always by paragraphs using the same basic sentence structures and vocabularies repeatedly and rhythmically.

The structure of *Two* is certainly much tighter than that of *The
Making of Americans*, not only because of the book's shorter length
and its continuous use of interlocking sentences and paragraphs, but
also because it does not indulge in long generalizations about psychological types. *Two*, however, does assume the same psychological
system established in the earlier book; and it continues to use many
of its terms, such as "attacking" and "resisting." But Stein no longer
bothers to define the words; she simply uses them. We find little of
the textbook in *Two*, nor do we find the style we saw in the latter
part of *A Long Gay Book*, where sense almost disappears in favor of
word play. The following passage is as close as *Two* comes to being

nonmimetic: "He had the alteration of the remaining wagon and he did not then feel that he had the skin that was burning when there was there what came to be there as he went in and out in swimming. He was not analogous" (128). But even here, we could, if we wished, puzzle out a meaning that might relate the passage to the rest of the book.

Two looks ahead to Stein's portraits by demanding that we know biographical facts in order to respond fully to the "content." If this insistence on her right to be completely personal in her writing is more than the average reader is willing to grant, it is still only an extreme symptom of the direction that most innovative writing has taken for almost two centuries. We could certainly read *Two* both pleasurably and profitably if we never knew the identity of any of its characters; it is the story of an evolving relationship among certain psychological types. In many ways, it is unfortunate that we have the title to lead us too closely back to "reality."

Most important, however, is the style that Stein develops in *Two* — that of the interlocking cinema technique which makes paragraphs tightly knit units and which meshes them to one another like the gears in a transmission. This style is the dominant one of the earliest portraits, a style that Stein was to use at continuous intervals throughout her career; it is a counterpoint to the word-play style developed in *A Long Gay Book* that dominates the later portraits.

III *Stein and Cubism*

Before focusing directly on the portraits and still lifes, we must consider briefly some relationships between Stein's new style of writing and the styles being developed in painting by her many friends in the artists' quarter. One advantage that the abstract painter, sculptor, and musician have over the literary artist is that the materials of their arts are less intrinsically mimetic than his. For the Modernist artist who wishes to create works not contingent on the reality of the external world, this fact is an obvious advantage. A Cubist painting, for instance, demands to be looked at, not interpreted. While such a painting may have within it certain features that ask the viewer to compare it with configurations in the world he knows — such as the fragmented features of a human face or body — the real problem it poses for the critic is not one of "meaning" but of finding a way to discuss form, mass, color, texture, and line.

Freed by their insights from the tyranny of perspective, Modernist painters declared that any obligation to create the illusion of depth

was only a convention, just like all the customs and traditions surrounding their art. A painting was merely color on a flat canvas, and
that is all it ever had been. Matisse and Picasso, Braque and Kan-
dinsky, attempted to convey their new sense of freedom with a
number of devices: by creating paintings with nonillusionistic, two-
dimensional flatness; by using colors in any way they liked (blue
trees and green noses); and by fragmenting formal configurations in
much the same way that the eye initially sees only parts of figures
before the mysterious process of memory and conceptual ordering
takes over and composes "reality" into familiar shapes.

Now, it is true that by using colors and lines the painter will
always arouse in the viewer some association from his empirical experience of the world. In this sense, he can never create a truly non-
contingent work of art that is purely itself and nothing else. But he
does, because of the nature of his materials, have a much greater opportunity to adopt the attitude that a person has only to look at his
work in order to experience it. His painting, given this attitude, can
be autonomous to a degree that no literary work can ever hope to be;
for words and letters — no matter how dislodged they are from
traditional continuities and because they make specific reference to
the world — demand that a reader call on his experience outside the
work of art. Since human beings are, after all, totally dependent on
language for any kind of self-consciousness, the literary artist simply
by using words is working with the basic reality of any reader;
therefore, his art can scarcely be as nonmimetic as the painter's.

Still, Stein wished to appropriate from the Cubist painters their attitude that, since they were free of the need to "put the mirror up to
reality," they could create autonomous artifacts. This attitude in
itself is a radical departure from previous attempts by writers to
mirror the effects of other art forms, such as the use of picturesque
language to paint word-pictures by late eighteenth- and early
nineteenth-century writers or E. M. Forster's celebrated rendering
of Beethoven's Fifth in *Howard's End* in the twentieth century. John
Malcolm Brinnin has described this attitude well in his critical
biography of Stein:

In most previous associations of poets and painters, and in all previous com-
parisons of their works, identifications and congruencies had for the most
part hinged upon similarities in subject matter and attitude. . . . When the
cubists jettisoned subject matter, liaisons between poetry and painting on
the old basis were no longer possible. . . . When the literary content of paint-

ing was omitted in favor of the freely conceived mathematical or intuitive exercise of purely plastic values, Gertrude Stein also attempted to drop subject matter in order to concentrate freely upon the "plastic" potentialities of language itself. (129)

Brinnin's observation is excellent, but I should like to caution the reader that the comparison of one art with another is at best a metaphor. The critic's job is not to look for the exact ways in which Stein's techniques correspond to those of Cubist painting. She did not try to "imitate" Picasso so crudely as that. What she opted for was the same freedom to dislocate the previous forms and conventions of the literary tradition in which she found herself. In using language "plastically," Stein wishes to create new literary structures and to pretend for the purposes of linguistic freshness that she is the first person ever to use particular words. Being, so to speak, the creator of the English language, Stein can therefore assign whatever meanings she likes to her words and to the sentences in which they appear.

Our emphasis, then, must not be on discovering the conventional "meaning" of any of her portraits or on finding the exact correspondences between her writing and Cubist painting. Instead, we must attempt to find some way of both describing and responding to what Stein was able to achieve in writing when she adopted the freedom that had belonged up to that time only to painters.

For Stein, as for the Cubists, a portrait was an occasion; and it did not constitute an obligation to copy its supposed subject. She began with her subject, sometimes only with its name; from there, she went on to create a verbal form; and the basis of its structure evolves from its internal relationships rather than from its echoes of the world external to it. True, there are elements even in the most obscure portrait that we can readily associate with its subject; and in some of the portraits there are more hints of "reality" than in others. But Stein's art, like that of the Cubists, is an art of the surface; and we will serve our enjoyment best by concentrating on her compositional innovations.

IV *The "Portraits"*

There are five basic varieties among Stein's portraits: (1) those that use the interlocking repetitions of *Two* — the cinema technique; (2) those that repeat the stylistic transition of *A Long Gay Book* from interlocking repetition to nonsemantic prose; (3) portraits composed of dialogue written without quotation marks; (4) series of *non sequiturs* in which individual sentences and paragraphs carry little traditional meaning, and which gain their effects primarily by oblique suggestiveness; and (5) poems using the *non-sequitur* style and depending for their surface texture on word play, puns, and the conventional auditory effects of poetry.[8]

In the first portrait type, written in the interlocking, repetitious style of *Two*, there is, as in its model, a relatively high degree of mimetic content. We always find a recognizable subject and usually a definite narrative line. Stein's first portrait, "Ada," which is told primarily in this style, is a straightforward, though stylized, summary of what we surmise to be Alice Toklas's relationships with her widower father and then with Gertrude Stein. What is immediately characteristic is Stein's euphemistic style, the style we have watched grow progressively more abstract. She uses only a few names, referring to herself simply as "someone." Consistent with what we have seen Stein do before, "Ada" presents general types and focuses on the *patterns* of events and emotions rather than on their specific details.

Since hundreds of Stein portraits have been published in a number of volumes, treatment of them must necessarily be selective. Among the many examples of the first variety are all those in *Two and Other Stories*,[9] as well as the famous first portrait of Picasso. Although it is difficult to date precisely all of Stein's writing, it seems to me that she developed the first portrait type earliest as an outgrowth of the longer works she was composing at the same time. As the style of *A Long Gay Book* underwent its transformation, so did the style of her portraits. The one of Picasso is especially interesting because of the way it threads three motifs through interlocking repetitions that slowly give a clear though generalized sense of the artist and his followers. Since it is too long to quote in full, I refer the reader to the reprint in the *Selected Writings of Gertrude Stein*.[10] A complete example of the first portrait type that can be quoted is entitled "Storyette H. M.," and the initials refer to Henri Matisse:

One was married to some one. That one was going away to have a good time. The one that was married to that one did not like it very well that the one to whom that one was married then was going off alone to have a good time and was leaving that one to stay at home then. The one that was going came in all glowing. The one that was going had everything he was needing to have the good time he was wanting to be having then. He came in all glowing. The one he was leaving at home to take care of the family living was not glowing. The one that was going was saying, the one that was glowing, the one that was going was saying then, I am content, you are not content, I am content you are not content, I am content, you are not content, you are content, I am content.[11]

Leon Katz has claimed that Stein based this portrait on a conversation she overheard between M. and Mme. Matisse.[12] She seems to have disapproved of the "brutal" way in which the painter treated his wife, and Katz therefore supposes she reproduced the conversation at the end of the portrait as a means of putting the great master in his place. However, Katz claims that Stein "confuses her point, and assigns the whole dialogue to Matisse" (124n). Does this mean we are to think less highly of the portrait because of its possible biographical inaccuracy? I maintain once again that it is irrelevant to worry about the biographical "truth" of any of Stein's writing. "Storyette H. M." is quite accessible as an autonomous unit of self-contained narrative; its characters could be almost any man and wife; its situation is familiar to most marriages. Only the tantalizing initials in the title invite biographical speculations, just as the subtitle and not the specific references of *Two* make us read that work as autobiography.

In "Storyette," we have once again a narrative in which no characters are named; for Stein uses the same generalized terms, such as "one." We do not know that this couple is heterosexual until the middle of the story when one character is finally identified as "he." Stein handles the interlocking repetitions subtly, without the heavy stylization of either.*The Making of Americans* or *Two*. In addition to using "one" in almost every sentence, Stein repeats such phrases as "one that was married," "one that was leaving," "good time," and "glowing." Her basic tools are the rhythms she builds through repetition and alternation, and the balance finally manages to suggest the psychological rhythms of not only two individuals but of one complex relationship. As a result, when we read the enigmatic, perhaps sarcastic conversation (without quotation marks) at the end, we seem to know the basic core of this relationship. If we worry about whether Stein really knew the Matisses well enough to be critical of them, we miss the point. By her technique of generalizing, Stein makes it possible to read this as an abstract portrait of the kind of relationship that is possible between two people of definite psychological types.

The second portrait variety has *A Long Gay Book* as its model: it begins in the style of interlocking repetition and then shifts almost totally into word play. A clear example is the "Portrait of Constance Fletcher" in *Geography and Plays*. A long portrait, it begins with the usual interlocking repetition in what seems to be a series of specific but generalized references to the titled subject:

> When she was quite a young one she knew she had been in a family living and that that family living was one that any one could be one not have been having if they were to be one being one not thinking about being one having been having family living. She was one then when she was a young one thinking about having, about having been having family living. She was one thinking about this thinking, she was one feeling thinking about this thing, she was one feeling being one who could completely have feeling in thinking about being one who had had, who was having family living.[13]

The interlocking repetitions continue for a few pages, along with an occasional new motif. And then the grounds of Stein's concentration shift as she moves from this style into word play and *non sequitur*. The final seven pages are a collection of puns, rhymes, and assorted rhythmic effects; for example:

> Oh the bells that are the same are not stirring and the languid grace is not out of place and the older fur is disappearing. There is not such an end. (159)

and

> This which did not escape was not the narrow connection that can make a larger blossom and make it take the sea where the ocean is larger and the ships are quicker. The pleasure is the same. (164)

This movement from the repetitive style used to categorize psychological types to the word-play style of the second variety of portraits mirrors not only the change in *A Long Gay Book* but also the general shift of Stein's style during the decade from *Q. E. D.* to *Tender Buttons*.

The third variety of portrait consists of dialogue written with neither quotation marks nor stage directions. An excellent example is "Mrs. Whitehead" (also in *Geography and Plays*) which is a moderately long, cryptic conversation between two distinct consciousnesses who are quite probably Mrs. Alfred North Whitehead (the philosopher's wife) and Gertrude Stein. Although it is difficult to isolate passages for quotation, the conversation does have a subject. The two speakers are discussing fairly ordinary, quotidian items such as homemaking, crocheting, and knitting. The conversation begins in the middle and continues with all the half-starts, *non sequiturs*, misunderstandings, and interruptions that one experiences in the average discussion. Some of the exchanges are quite funny:

> I can be careful.
> Not within wearing it.
> I cannot say to stay.
> No please don't get up.
> And now that.
> Yes I see. (155)

This kind of portrait prefigures what Stein does in her "plays" and "operas." A kind of absurdist dialogue, Stein wrote it years before either Samuel Beckett or Eugene Ionesco wrote similar exchanges in their dramas.

The fourth portrait type presents from the beginning a steady series of *non sequiturs*. The famous — and, during its time, notorious — "Portrait of Mabel Dodge at the Villa Curonia" is an example. Written while Gertrude and Alice were visiting Mabel Dodge at her Italian estate, its title celebrates the moment of the portrait's composition. After its famous opening line — "The days are wonderful and the nights are wonderful and the life is pleasant."[14] — we find only minor suggestions of either the Villa Curonia or Mabel Dodge. The author is excited about being where she is, and her mode of expression is to use the language with all her assumed freedom to treat only the surface, to write about the simplest things naively perceived, and to make full use of puns and word play. As a matter of fact, Stein is supposed to have written the portrait in a single sitting.

Since the "Portrait of Mabel Dodge" defies easy quotation, I have chosen the shorter, "Eric de Haulleville," which exhibits the same qualities: "Charles has got a goat he has taught how to keep it in a boat which is why they marry if they want to they have now not changed for Wednesday it is partly at a large enlargement that they can do without help which is made to be at twenty which is four. How old are twenty eight more for themselves. In wedded welcome theirs admire. It is partly lain down."[15]

Once again, the identity of Eric de Haulleville makes no

difference. This may be a marriage poem since "marry" appears in the first and "wedded" in the next-to-last sentence. But the portrait is certainly not some kind of Cubist "epithalamion." It has none of the characteristics commonly associated with the marriage song.[16] Since it also contains neither continuous narrative nor a logically structured argument, "Eric de Haulleville" directs our attention to the pattern of linguistic associations by which it achieves its particular formal unity. We find the echo of "goat" in "boat," the repetition of "wh" sounds, "now not," "large enlargement," "four" and "more," "wedded welcome," and "twenty" is repeated twice. Rhymes, assonance, echo: is it merely nonsense? In semantic terms, yes; it is non-sense. But the same kind of over-determination of sounds found in most poetry distinguishes "Eric de Haulleville" from traditional prose and subtly ties together its various parts even though they do not make any "sense."

The logical extension of this style to the portrait written in actual verse form constitutes the fifth variety. Some of these portrait-poems, such as "Susie Asado" and "Preciosilla" ("Toasted Susie is my ice-cream"), have achieved a minor notoriety; but, since they are a bit long, I shall discuss the poem "Kristians Tonny"(1929):

Better than without it. It is not the same as the.
The hope it is in the hope of it. It is better than without.
Might be why they asked to have the handles.
It, it is usual to add rose which is four rows. It is usual
to add it.[17]

Although Tonny was both a painter of minor reputation and a friend of Stein's, neither historical fact plays a recognizable role in the poem. The tone has the ring of casual, interrupted conversation, but the biographical connotations, if there are any, are too private to concern us. "Kristians Tonny" is a simple poem, so simple that its dominant word is "it." There is a surprise at the end of the first line when, at the end of the second sentence, the word "the" leads us to believe that it will be followed by a noun. But that is typical of Stein's linguistic surprises, for "the" functions not as an article but as a noun itself since parts of speech are determined in English by syntax and not morphology.

When we begin, however, to question how the various parts of speech function in any linguistic utterance, we leave ourselves open to a polysemous situation in which a sentence can have an infinite number of meanings. Suppose, for instance, I am wrong about the opening line of "Kristians Tonny" — suppose that it is intentionally unfinished and that a period is consciously used at the end instead of the expected ellipsis. If this supposition is correct, the second line becomes the hesitant continuation of the thought at the end of the first. We would then have to read the lines in this way: "It is not the same as the . . the hope [that] it is in the hope of it." But we could also suppose that this reading is wrong and that, instead, "it" in the second line is the subject of the sentence and "hope" simply modifies "it." It is easy to see into what a linguistic slough of despond we would fall if we troubled ourselves too much with the *sense* of the lines. In treating language so cavalierly, Stein runs the danger of a maddening polysemy; but, in return for taking this chance, she achieves the great pleasure of showing that language can be turned into a plastic instrument stripped of meaning by any writer or speaker who is willing to tamper with its traditional linguistic structures. Stein, more than Joyce or any other writer I can think of, can show us just what ambiguous possibilities are inherent in language.

The kind of Alexandrianism that Stein manifests is most typical during times of great cultural crisis when writers are most liable to consider their language a corrupt instrument with which to transmit a corrupt culture. It is no accident that many writers of the early twentieth century had similar attitudes toward their own language. T. S. Eliot's Prufrock feels himself drowning in a sea of human voices; for, like Stein, Eliot also felt himself born into a time of great cultural and linguistic corruption. That he did not seek Stein's particular way of trying to "purify" the language does not invalidate either of their perceptions or quests.

What "Kristians Tonny" ultimately leads us to is a philosophical contemplation on the ultimate inadequacy of language to convey anything through the accumulated meanings of words. If we couple this contemplation with the joys inherent in the music of verbal sounds, then we shall receive the highly special kind of pleasure that only Stein's attack on the entire history of the English language can give us. That the implications of what she was doing did not escape her is made clear by the philosophical contemplations she later composed about the meanings of grammar, poetry, and linguistic experimentation — ideas we shall consider in a later chapter.

At any rate, the verbal freedom that Stein developed and maintained in her portraits was as far as she was to go in that direction for the rest of her life. The extreme limits of her style were established by the time of World War I, and they form the basis of all her experiments in form from that time on in poetry, drama, fiction, philosophy, and reminiscence.

V   Tender Buttons

One curious Stein work we must discuss briefly before moving on to her work in drama is the little book of still lifes called *Tender Buttons*. These sketches represent another movement toward a more total abstractionism, although it is not a stylistic choice but one of subject. *Tender Buttons* shows a shift in focus from people to things, as was the case with so much modern painting. It has always been assumed that the writer must deal with human problems; but, in following the model of the painter's freedom of subject matter, Stein decided that the writer could also exercise his art on anything, no matter how simple and seemingly insignificant. *Tender Buttons* is Stein's celebration of the trivial, by which I do not in the least mean to suggest that it is trivial itself.

Both Leon Katz and Allegra Stewart have suggested that at the bottom of Stein's interest in the trivial lies a mystic religiosity. While I am not wholly convinced that this suggestion is true, it is worth serious consideration. There is much evidence of Stein's genuine interest in saints, particularly in Saint Theresa of Avila in *Four Saints in Three Acts*. There is also Stein's collection, *Portraits and Prayers*. What she always found remarkable about the saintly was their serene simplicity. That she had the same image of herself provides an interesting metaphor with which to interpret so simple and primitive an art of the surface and of the celebration of the ordinary as we find in *Tender Buttons*. Katz concludes his thesis by saying that Stein's "unique art subsequently emerged as an endlessly full hymn of pleasure in the actual, a nonselective tribute to the uniform splendors of existence."[18] Stewart suggests "that *Tender Buttons* should be regarded as a mandala, a 'magic circle' or enclosure for the unconscious mind, originating in its maker's unconscious but elaborated, with more or less conscious purpose, as an act of self-creation."[19] There is really nothing to take issue with in Katz's remarks; and, although we could easily disagree with Stewart's use of Jungian analytic categories in the first half of her statement, her claim in the latter half seems to take account admirably of Stein's creative process; and we shall return to these considerations in a moment.

Tender Buttons is divided into three sections, "Objects," "Food," and "Rooms"; the first two contain a series of short prose poems and the final one is an extended prose poem composed in paragraphs. It is generally not possible to gloss the various poems by relating their semantic content to their titles. As with the portraits, these still lifes are occasions for the author to make general reflections that are triggered by the objects referred to in the title but that are not descriptive of them. Here is an example:

A RED STAMP
    If lilies are lily white if they exhaust noise and distance and even dust, if they dusty will dirt a surface that has no extreme grace, if they do this and it is not necessary it is not at all necessary if they do this they need a catalogue.[20]

Such an utterance almost totally defies conventional literary interpretation, and the critic who attempts an ingenious gloss only leaves himself open to contradiction with almost every statement. Even so, occasional lines in *Tender Buttons* make some tantalizing, though oblique, reference to their supposed subject:

RED ROSES
    A cool red rose and a pink cut pink, a collapse and a sold hole, a little less hot. (472)

Julian Sawyer has composed an interpretation of this still life whose tentativeness he admits;[21] but beyond the explicitness of the opening phrase and the color pink that appears next, the context forces him to suggest such tenuous readings as "collapse" meaning a vase. Before "sold hole," my mind begins to boggle. Is it a vase that is "sold"? Once again, such glossing is silly. If we accept the outrageous metaphor in the title, tender buttons, and move from there to such linguistic playthings as "sold hole," we begin to see that Stein is playing a Wittgensteinian language game, if only to discover what the limits of her language really are.

    Stein is doing just what the Cubist painters were trying to do with the language of their art: test its limits. Most critics, including this one, have treated *Tender Buttons* as a prose equivalent of Cubism; and this approach still seems a valid one for an immensely puzzling work. Stein expressed an admiration for the surface art of painting that suggests quite strongly her wish that we pay the same attention to her own verbal collage. In "Pictures," one of the *Lectures in*

America, she says: "any oil painting whether it is intended to look like something and looks like it or whether it is intended to look like something and does not look like it it really makes no difference, the fact remains that for me it has achieved an existence in and for itself, it exists on as being an oil painting on a flat surface and it has its own life and like it or not there it is and I can look at it and it does hold my attention."(61)

By analogy, *Tender Buttons* is a series of black symbols on a white page; its symbols are letters which, when combined, become words, and the combination of words becomes sentences. We know there are sentences because periods appear every now and then, and we know that the sentences become paragraphs because of the periodic incidence of indentations. These dark figures are there to attract attention, to be looked at and appreciated for what they are to the eye and to the elementary processes of the mind. We are to admire, along with the author, the wonders of creation and to join her in what seems like the initial naming of the parts that make up the totality of that creation which she has called *Tender Buttons.* "In the beginning was the Word." If the world consists of nothing but language, then Stein feels that her function is to use that language with the freshness of a child. She substantiates this contention in *Lectures in America:*

And then, something happened and I began to discover the names of things, that is not discover the names but discover the things the things to see the things to look at and in so doing I had of course to name them not to give them new names but to see that I could find out how to know that they were there by their names or by replacing their names. And how was I to do so. They had their names and naturally I called them by the names they had and in doing so having begun looking at them I called them by their names with passion and that made poetry, I did not mean it to make poetry but it did, it made the Tender Buttons, and the Tender Buttons was very good poetry it made a lot more poetry, and I will now more and more tell about that and how it happened. ("Poetry and Grammar,"235)

It is not necessary to analyze in detail any passages from *Tender Buttons* because the linguistic and poetic techniques employed there are the same that we have seen throughout the portraits, and because a number of detailed studies to which the reader may refer exist.[22] What I wish to do is explore briefly the hypothesis set forth by Allegra Stewart, who, as has been suggested, sees Stein as an ultimately religious writer and *Tender Buttons* as an extended meditation in the form of a mandala. Stewart does not mean to suggest that Stein participated in any form of religious worship, for Stein rejected all other-worldly beliefs. Stewart quotes from Alfred North Whitehead to give authority to her use of the word: "religion is what the individual does with his solitariness"(133); and "expression is the one fundamental sacrament" (14).

According to Stewart, *Tender Buttons* is the product of extended contemplations during which Stein developed her own individuation by bringing to the surface through *conscious* effort the structures of her unconscious which were essential keys to what Stein might have called her "bottom nature." Miss Stewart's Jungian concepts, however, lead us beyond personality (the seat of Stein's "human nature") to an area that Stein was later to call "mind,"[23] in which the categories of essential being exist for all mankind. This sense of a kind of collective unconscious that is discoverable only through contemplation and recollection is what Stewart claims is the key to understanding the mandala structure of *Tender Buttons*.

By mandala, Stewart means "a formalized circular design — containing or contained by a figure of three, four, or five points of emphasis" (110). There was a mandala of sorts printed on the cover of the first edition of *Tender Buttons*, but there is no reason to believe that Stein either designed the cover or understood the significance of the design. The mandala is actually a device used in Eastern magic, "a magic circle": "The picture has the obvious purpose of drawing a *sulcus primigenius*, a magical furrow, around the centre, the *templum*, or *temenos* (sacred precincts), of the innermost personality, in order to prevent 'emanation,' or to guard by apotropaeic means, deflections through external influences" (111). In serious contemplation, the truth of the inner personality and of what that personality has in common with the world-mind emerges; and this emergence has supposedly occurred in *Tender Buttons*.

Stewart attempts to show the extreme unity of *Tender Buttons* by an extended etymological analysis of its Indo-European word roots, but this analysis seems an unconvincing rationalization of a point already made. It need not be necessary, however, to accept its extremities to find such a point of view useful. Stein's writing did take on an increasingly contemplative character as she came to regard herself more and more as both a genius and a saint. She seemed to need the saintly simplicity of her primitivist prose to express best the most profound truths of her unconscious personality and mind. The incantatory qualities of much of her prose lead us to read her in quite this way.

Because Stein came to rely so much on the validity of her own consciousness as the sole means of communing with the world, she ceased to care about the differences between literary works that succeed or fail or about the kinds of literary taste that govern most critical judgments. She ceased to rewrite, and she began to allow anything into her work that managed to find its way into her consciousness. Thornton Wilder describes this development well in his "Introduction" to *Four in America:*

> She introduces what I like to call "the irruption of the daily life." If her two dogs are playing at her feet while she is writing she puts them into the text. She may suddenly introduce some phrases she has just heard over the garden wall. This resembles a practice that her friends the Post-impressionist painters occasionally resorted to. They pasted a subway ticket to the surface of their painting. The reality of a work of art is one reality; the reality of a "thing" is another reality; the juxtaposition of the two kinds of reality gives a bracing shock. It also insults the reader; but the reader is not present, nor even imagined. It refreshes in the writer the sense that the writer is all alone, alone with his thoughts and his struggle and even with his relation to the outside world that lies about him.[24]

The progression from a narrative consciousness that takes part in telling and manipulating a tale to a consciousness that expresses nothing but its own continuous flow of thought, feeling, and perception has turned finally into the kind of total egocentric reliance on self that is one logical outcome of the Romantic world-view. All consciousness during such egoistic contemplation is a continuous surprise because memory and convention do not force it into any patterns other than those controlled by its own internal structures. "Surprise," Stein says near the end of *Tender Buttons,* "the only surprise has no occasion. It is an ingredient and the section the whole section is one season" (509). Whatever "immediate data of consciousness"[25] come to mind during her contemplation are sufficient for her to transmit to the page; for language, no matter how carefully used, can never adequately describe the contents of human consciousness.

This total trust in self, so like the serenity of the saint, whether or not it is religious in either origin or sensibility, is characteristic of Stein's personality and writing from the time of the portraits, and especially of *Tender Buttons,* onward. We shall do well to keep these qualities in mind as we continue to tour her consciousness.

CHAPTER 5

Operas and Plays

I *The Major Periods of Stein's Career*

THE publication of *Tender Buttons* on the eve of World War I provides a convenient breaking point in discussing Stein's development. For the best part of the next two decades Stein elaborated on the innovations of her early period in a series of works in all genres, including the novel, the drama, poetry, and many extended "portraits," "landscapes," and "geographies." With the exceptions of the opera *Four Saints in Three Acts* (written in 1927) and perhaps the essay "Composition as Explanation" (1926), most of what Stein wrote during this time is almost unknown to the reading public. That does not indicate, however, that what she did for almost two decades is unimportant. To the contrary. Although Stein did her most innovative writing during the first decade and a half of this century, she composed in her second and third periods many of her most accomplished works — works that are, however, still almost completely unread.

In her second period, Stein became even more heavily concerned with the nature of human identity and with theories of the development of twentieth-century culture. Particularly in her plays, but also in "Composition as Explanation," she showed her overriding interest in such matters. Ironically, the latter work is one of the few she wrote at that time that is both discursive and "comprehensible," but the fact that it was first delivered as a lecture explains much of its communicative directness. The semi-explanatory prose of this essay prepares the way for what is to be the dominant style of Stein's third major period.

During this final period, which lasted until her death in 1946, Stein produced some of her most well-known works; she became comprehensible primarily to indulge in a lifelong need for explanation that she had until now expressed mostly in conversation.

Although she was to continue composing in "Steinese" the rest of her life, she began in 1932 to write a series of extended works of theory, criticism, fiction, drama, and autobiography that any reader can understand. The major foci of these writings continue to be human nature and identity as well as the justification of Stein's own position in Modernist culture. As an older woman, Stein felt an overpowering need for justification and recognition after a lifetime of both notoriety and personal obscurity. Ironically, however, the popular success of *The Autobiography of Alice B. Toklas* in 1933, and the American lecture tour that followed almost immediately, threatened Stein's own carefully honed sense of identity by turning her overnight into a public figure. She discusses the consternation of dealing with her sudden fame most interestingly in *Everybody's Autobiography* (1937).

To work properly with the vast amount of material Stein wrote from the time of the composition of *Tender Buttons* to the end of her career, we shall deal with her work by genres rather than try to cover successively everything she wrote during a specific period. Also, since Stein's output was so immense (forty volumes or so), a critical book of modest length must be somewhat selective. While we shall discuss a large proportion of what Stein wrote, we shall of necessity stress those works that are either well known or are particularly important for a rounded understanding of Stein's development. We shall devote an entire chapter to Stein's operas and plays since they are the major belletristic achievement of her later career and since her output in this genre was quite large; another chapter considers Stein's work in the novel; and the final chapter deals with the writings most well known to the general public — her works of nonfictional prose in criticism, theory, philosophy, and autobiography. Every chapter, however, although limited to the discussion of particular genres, deals with the works both chronologically and within the context of the various periods of Stein's career.

II *Early Drama*

The first "drama" Stein wrote was "What Happened, A Five Act Play" (1913). Published in 1922 in *Geography and Plays,* it exemplifies the spirit of playfulness that generated many of Stein's experiments in the portraits and in *Tender Buttons.* The generic name "play" is quite apt because the dramatic form gave Stein the proper outlet to play out fully the drama of human personality and its interaction with landscape.[1] And, as usual, Stein uses genres in order to question their validity. The fact that "What Happened" is called a "play" warns us to prepare those expectations we bring to the reading of any drama. She reinforces our generic set by dividing the play into five explicitly labelled acts. There is, however, nothing further that we can recognize as a dramatic convention. The names of no characters appear to the left of lines of dialogue. There is, in fact, nothing that resembles a speech, not even the kind of minimally recognizable conversation we found in the third portrait variety, which is composed of dialogue written without quotation marks. Moreover, no stage directions appear; and there is no action, either explicit or implicit.

What then makes "What Happened" a play other than the fact that Stein calls it one? In one sense at least, nothing; for it is possible to give anything — even a telephone book — a dramatic reading. Here, as elsewhere, Stein transforms the traditional orientation of a literary genre; in this case, the transformation is from the drama of interacting characters created through their spoken lines to what is usually considered a secondary element of the drama — the background or, as Stein would have said, the landscape or geography. Consonant with her shift from people to objects in her portraits is this shift from the human drama enacted against a background to the background turned into a foreground that can exist dramatically with or without people.

As a result, Stein's play exists primarily in the mood generated by words that create a sense of environment. She uses in "What Happened" the verbal techniques of the fourth portrait variety, the juxtaposition of poetic *non sequiturs;* and any search for the "sense" of the words is obviously quixotic. The implications of this kind of *jeu d'esprit* become more apparent as we examine Stein's work in this genre, a genre she in many ways invents, just as she creates unique forms for all her work.[2]

Stein worked out her attitudes toward the drama in a series of short plays first published in *Geography and Plays.* As usual, she explored the experimental possibilities of this genre as soon as she decided to "invent" it for herself. There are several varieties of Stein plays just as there are a number of portrait types. Rather than try to isolate them schematically, we shall run through several of Stein's early "one-acters" to see the kinds of innovations embodied in each. But, before doing so, we must consider the general implications of her dramatic experiments.[3]

Stein exhibits two major fascinations in her "plays." One is with the sound of human voices; the other, with establishing the setting for whatever action or inaction occurs in the course of human living and being. Many plays simply string together bits of dialogue in the *non sequitur* style of her portraits. The characters — either named or simply voices — speak lines often remarkably mimetic of actual speech, with witty juxtapositions that remind us of the theater of Beckett and Ionesco. But the composition of the physical world is equally important to her, for speech to Stein is an action that takes place during time and that emanates from the mouths of characters existing within space. It is best, then, to view her plays as "landscapes" or "geographies" in which characters move and where speech can be heard. I say "speech" rather than "dialogue" because the latter implies a communicative interaction between speakers, and this kind of relationship is rarely evident in Stein's dramas; but voices are always heard, and landscape is always somehow presented.

As we have already seen, Stein not only does not use the terms of drama conventionally, but she applies these terms any way she chooses. She places acts within scenes, calls one line of unlabelled dialogue an act, names a series of *non-sequitur* monologues a play. Why not? The terms of drama are normally instructional devices for actors, directors, and audiences, even though we tend to think of them as constitutive to the very nature of the theater. What Stein forces us to understand is that the labels "play," "act," and "scene" are conventional forms of learned behavior for both creator and perceiver, much as perspective — the so-called painterly necessity rediscovered during the Renaissance — was for four hundred years of Western culture. Once such conventions are seen as only conventions, they can be manipulated by anyone who wishes to do so.

Stein also wishes us to meditate about the radical meanings of these labelling words. As I have already suggested, Stein's use of the word "play" has to do not just with drama but with *playing*, with *homo ludens*. Her own language is playful, as is her arbitrary use of traditional dramatic structures and expectations. For Stein, an *act* is not just a division of a play, a room in a house; an act has to do with *act*ing, with verbal *act*ions performed by "characters played by *act*ors. A scene is not just a division of an act; it is a place that can be *seen*, a landscape, a piece of geography, the setting where life goes on and where words are spoken, but where nothing necessarily "happens." Indeed, until the plays she wrote in the last decade of her career, nothing at all does happen in any conventional sense of that word.

The truth is that Stein has no interest in dramatic progression, which is, after all, just another theatrical convention. People live lives, not dramas. The individual life has no systolic-diastolic cycle; it achieves form only through self-consciousness and art. Life is a series of varied, ritualized repetitions; as Stein suggests in "Composition as Explanation," repetitions compose the essence of what we are. Stein's "plays" are in this sense best understood as rituals that are strictly formalized by a mind that tends to see the world abstractly and statically. There is no action *per se* in these plays; there are only gestures, a situation much in keeping with Stein's theories of psychological types in which individual actions are of interest only in the ways they exemplify abstract principles.

Stein's interest in the theater extended back to her childhood. The dramatic experiences that seem to have meant most to her were operas and melodramas, both of them highly formulaic modes of theater. In operas, which for American audiences are almost always sung in a foreign language, the "meaning" of the lines of dialogue is rarely at issue. Although the audience usually knows the general plot outline, the specific "speeches" are not vehicles to advance a story as much as occasions to hear words sung to music.

In addition, Stein's interest in both Shakespeare and the bullfights reinforced her instinct for the drama's ritualized aspects. The theatergoer at a performance of *Hamlet* does not concern himself much with the story's mystery aspects, any more than the Athenian did when he watched *Oedipus Tyrannus.*We know the Dane's story already and are quite prepared to watch the millionth staging of the Prince of Denmark's tragedy; and we demand only that the ritual be enacted with competence, dignity, and style. The bullfight *aficionado* knows that in almost all cases the bull will die and the matador live; therefore, his major concern is that the latter so enact the ritual of death as to create in the spectator a properly transcendent emotion, much as the celebrant must do when performing the ritual of the bread and the wine.

Given the stylized aspects of Stein's plays, the area of greatest tension and interest, aside from their staging by various directors, continues to be their use of word play. But the reader who has followed the growing abstractionism of Stein's style to this point finds little that is linguistically new in any of her dramas. What this new form does is provide Stein's linguistic inventiveness with a new setting — a new area in which she can help the English language regain its lost freshness. Her formal experimentation in the short works in *Geography and Plays* shows the steady evolution of the dramatic form that finally astonished the American theater in *Four Saints in Three Acts*. The varieties of what Stein is willing to call a play seem at times almost infinite.

For instance, "White Wines" (1913) contains no action, no dialogue, no act and scene divisions. Beneath the title — the usual place for listing the characters of a play — we find:

1. All together
2. Witnesses
3. House to house.
   (5 women)[4]

Hardly a list of characters! The play that follows consists of a series of paragraphs divided by phrases that are usually italicized and that are drawn from but do not correspond exactly to the lines that succeed the title. The contents of the paragraphs are similar to the flip, *non-sequitur* descriptions contained in *Tender Buttons*. They are either landscapes or still lifes, and they are verbally Cubist in structure. The only element of traditional theater Stein retains is that of setting. "White Wines" is a play because Stein calls it a play, not because it fulfills anything that even remotely resembles a handbook definition of drama.

In "Do Let Us Go Away" (1916), Stein attempts to see if a play can still retain its generic classification without any physical setting. This piece is composed completely of speeches, and the characters' names appear in parentheses flush against the left margin. There are no scenes or acts. The speeches are discontinuous in their responses to one another, much like "absurdist" dialogue. There is some conventional characterization since some of the names use their *non sequiturs* in what amounts to a pattern, but the "characters" are still primarily only names. In this play, however, we can at least identify the speakers of the various lines.

In "For the Country Entirely" (1916), subtitled "A Play in Letters," Stein writes a dramatic piece that is again without setting; it exists totally as discontinuous dialogue that is not linked by name to any character. The play is divided into arbitrary scenes and acts whenever Stein seems to feel the need for a break. The speeches consist primarily of the chit-chit we associate with polite society — the clichés of civilized intercourse into which Stein thrusts the introductions and signatures of what are supposed to be letters. The whole business is reminiscent of Jonathan Swift's *Polite Conversations*, a scathing though ultimately soporific satire of eighteenth-century manners. An enterprising director could probably mount an entertaining production of "For the Country Entirely," although he would have to decide somewhat arbitrarily who would speak what lines, a decision Virgil Thomson faced when writing the music to *Four Saints*.

The most playful piece in *Geography and Plays* is "Counting Her Dresses" (1917). It is divided into Parts, with each Part consisting of Acts. Only a few of the acts have more than one line, the longest being part 1, act 1, which has three. There are forty-one parts in "Counting Her Dresses" and perhaps one hundred and fifty acts. This is as far as Stein goes in demonstrating the absurdity of conventional theatrical labels, but the lesson has been the same throughout *Geography and Plays:* a play is any piece of writing the author wishes to call a play. Generic names exist only as psychological directions for the performers and the audience, and our expectations of what a play or a novel is supposed to be cause us to be so disoriented by what Stein presents us. As is always the case in Modernist art, the discovery that the "absolutes" are only conventions leads Stein to create her own conventions in everything she writes. That her originality is often exhausting and even tiresome does not change the fact that she always works against received convention and creates her own rules as she goes along. Still, her own conventions are so integral to her work that she seems ironically almost a classical writer with a rigid sense of decorum that is continuously functional from work to work. We shall now see how these conventions operate in Stein's full-length dramas.

III   Capital Capitals

After *Geography and Plays*, Stein published two collections of drama, *Operas and Plays* (1932) and *The Gertrude Stein First Reader and Three Plays* (1946); and, after her death, there appeared *Last Operas and Plays* (1949). A convenient and available selection of most of Stein's memorable drama appears in *Selected Operas and Plays of Gertrude Stein*, edited by John Malcolm Brinnin,[5] which includes three or four plays from each of Stein's collections of drama. In the remainder of this chapter we shall consider the following major plays and "operas": *Capital Capitals* (1922) and *Four Saints in Three Acts* (1927) from *Operas and Plays; Doctor Faustus Lights the Lights* (1938) and *The Mother of Us All* (1946) from *Last Operas and Plays;* and *Yes Is For a Very Young Man* (1946) from *The Gertrude Stein First Reader and Three Plays.*

Capital Capitals was set to music by Virgil Thomson, and we dis-

cuss it first because it now seems clear that Stein's major con-
tributions to the drama are her "operas" rather than her "plays."
Capital Capitals is the earliest of her works to be set to music,
although not the first to be staged as an opera. Stein's ritualistically
repetitive dramas fit almost perfectly the needs of the operatic com-
poser. The speeches are simple and rhythmic, they contain much internal rhyme, and they repeat. *Capital Capitals*, a short work, is
memorable primarily because of Thomson's charming score. Written
in the key of C for "four men and a piano,"[6] it contains little in the
way of harmony and only minor chording in a piano score that
follows note for note the words sung by the performers.

The script opens with an overture in the form of a chorus, in which
the puns inherent in the title are exploited. The references for the
word "capital" range from money to the seats of governments in
various countries. Once the punning is over, we witness the
emergence of the actual capitals which are to be the characters in the
opera. These are the capitals of Provence - Aix, Arles, Avignon, and
Les Baux — which are cast by Thomson as two tenors, a "baryton
[sic]," and a bass. They sing, often in rounds and in simple counterpoint, about everyday matters that might have some minimal relation to the "essence" of life in that particular capital or section of the
country.

In this sense, the characters conform to the convention of
landscape that Stein has already explored so often in her plays. The
talk is highly ritualized, the word play is continuous, the subject
matter of the conversation is simple to the point of triviality. This is
an opera that could be sung without costuming or sets. I do not know
how it has been staged, but it seems to me that *Capital Capitals*
could be performed simply by having the four singers and the pianist
appear with no properties other than the scores and the pianoforte.

IV   Four Saints in Three Acts

Perhaps someone could also stage *Four Saints in Three Acts* in
such a way, but the elaborate Broadway production is by now so
legendary that the opera will always be associated in the minds of
theatergoers with a kind of baroque opulence. The quartet of
capitals becomes in this work ostensibly a quartet of saints, but from
that point on most resemblances cease except for the fact that
idiosyncratic language pervades both.

The story of *Four Saints* is, like that of most Stein works of this
period, difficult to summarize as a coherent plot; but the "action" of

this opera-play is quite simple. There are actually more than four saints, although there are only two central ones, Saint Teresa of Avila and Saint Ignatius Loyola; and, in terms of emphasis, the play really belongs to Saint Teresa. The text consists of a series of meditations, primarily made by the narrator-chorus (Gertrude Stein) and some by the chorus of saints; and the meditations are mostly about sainthood and about the simple yet metaphysical problems of landscape and everyday life. The entire play is replete with the wise-child wit of the author and with word play that is often reminiscent of the portraits.

Halfway through, Stein introduces Saint Ignatius, although the narrator's hesitations clearly indicate that Stein was not so interested in him as in Saint Teresa. After a further series of simplistic meditations, Saint Ignatius and the chorus of saints sing the famous aria, "Pigeons in the grass alas." It is possible to read into the events of *Four Saints* much religious significance, although it is not obligatory to do so. There are plays on numbers; the pigeons seem to reflect Saint Francis (a saint who does not appear); there are also many reflections on sainthood and simplicity. Stein's religious sense, as always, has to do with what is apparent to the simplest perceptions, particularly to the sense of sight. In reality, however, the play is an extended meditation about the problems of being, and it is not a developed set of actions; for it to work, it must be a visual and an auditory spectacle, much as it seems to have been presented in its first performance. Otherwise, it is very undramatic drama.

Stein wrote *Four Saints* in actual collaboration with Virgil Thomson, a situation that gave her some problems. The cooperative effort is also a problem for the critic who must sort out what part of the opera is Stein's original version and what evolved from Thomson's adaptation of her text. In the notes to the RCA Victor Red Seal recording of *Four Saints*, Thomson claims that, although Stein advised him to do whatever he had to to make the script workable for the stage, "Actually I made no cuts or repeats in my first version. I put everything to music, even the stage directions, because they made such lovely lines for singing. Later I did make some cuts, with the advice of Maurice Grosser, who had added a scenario, or plot, to facilitate the staging. That scenario pleased Miss Stein."[7] The text of the recording is abridged, but the play as performed was not really shortened very much. The principal changes were the substitution of a chorus for the voice of the author, whose mind in the printed version presided over the opera's continuous composition, and Thomson's addition of a *compère* and *commère* (technically godparents, but really confidantes) to speak some of the lines of narration.

In staging, the major elaboration was the use of an all-black cast in an opera with Spanish characters. Thomson says that he "had chosen them purely for beauty of voice, clarity of enunciation, and fine carriage. Their surprise gift to the production was their understanding of the work. They got the spirit of it, enjoyed its multiple meanings, even its obscurities, adopted it, moved in on it." In addition, the production had Florine Stettheimer's famous cellophane scenery, was choreographed and directed by Frederick Ashton and John Houseman, and the orchestra was conducted by Alexander Smallens. A highly distinguished group of collaborators! The new American opera ran for more than sixty performances. It was a major musical event.

According to Richard Bridgman's judgment, "*Four Saints in Three Acts* occupies a more important position in Gertrude Stein's canon than its intrinsic worth can justify."[8] It is difficult to accept or refute this assessment since *Four Saints* has by now an almost mythical reputation and because, like any staged play, it is not just the product of its author. Stein obviously had trouble collaborating. For someone so individualistic, she must surely have bridled at the boring task of sticking all the way through a work to a preconceived subject. It was Thomson's suggestion that the opera be about saints and hers that the setting be Spain, a country she and Alice Toklas loved deeply and the place where she wrote *Tender Buttons* as well as a number of her early plays. The choice of two sixteenth-century Spanish saints, Saint Teresa of Avila and Saint Ignatius Loyola, the founder of the Jesuits, who did not so far as we can determine know each other, did not, according to Thomson, seem either to him or to Stein "an inconvenience." What was obviously difficult for Stein, however, was adhering to the "subject," which in actuality amounts to nothing more than the Spanish saints in their landscape.

In one sense, Stein's interest in saints should not surprise us because, for her, a saint was the truly fulfilled person who had to do nothing at all. He or she only had to be. In that sense, the saint is like Stein's conception of a landscape; it is the essence of a particular time and place. As she said in *Lectures in America*, "In Four Saints I made the Saints the landscape. All the saints that I made and I made a number of them because after all a great many pieces of things are in a landscape all these saints together made my landscape. These attendant saints were the landscape and it the play really is a landscape" (128 - 29). For the Christian, a saint is at the "still point of the turning world,"[9] having learned, like T. S. Eliot's penitent, to sit still. With her Cubist interest in essences. Stein could merge saints and a place into a single landscape; for the essence of place is created by a poet meditating on matters of structure and essence.

Stein's treatment of her subject may offend the tastes of some. There is a scene in which the saints play croquet, another where photographs are taken (the two saints lived in the sixteenth century). We must remember that Western religion has its own peculiar notions of decorum. Just three years before the writing of *Four Saints*, E. M. Forster had presented a similar situation in *A Passage to India*. In the celebrated conclusion to that novel, the pious Brahmin, Professor Godbole, allows butter to melt on his forehead in the middle of a religious ceremony celebrating the birth of God. There is no breach of decorum here because to the Hindu everything is possible within God's creation. So the viewer of *Four Saints* should not be upset by the notion of cellophane settings or of blacks playing the parts of Caucasian saints who play croquet. For Stein, as for essential Christianity, sainthood is a frame of mind, an attitude or perhaps a beatitude, but not a role with inviolably pristine standards of behavior.

The opera opens with a Prologue in which the chorus-narrator announces the subject with words redolent of Christian symbolism ("Love," "Saints," "fish"). The narrator — really Stein, the author — continually gives herself directions about what kind of a "narrative" she wants to be writing: "A narrative of prepare for saints in narrative prepare for saints."[10] Her hesitancy about getting to the actual saints and their essences makes it sound as though she is going through a series of five-finger exercises. In this regard, *Four Saints*, although an "opera," has much the same kind of narrative consciousness as Stein's "fictional" prose. Because she saw literary creation as a continuously extemporized series of moments, she always made the "subject" of her work the contents of her consciousness as expressed by the narrative voice. This procedure is also true of *Four Saints* in which there is no plot, no authorially indicated stage action beyond the most minimally oblique suggestions, no story, no resolution, no reversal, and no climax, either situational or thematic. Once again, Stein's major device for conveying her sense of structural essence is the meandering voice of her own consciousness.

Because it is impossible to isolate a paraphrasable plot from the text of *Four Saints*, a successful production depends heavily on whoever adapts it to the stage. For the American premiere, Maurice Grosser was given the task of constructing a scenario out of an already completed libretto and score. This scenario was reprinted along with the complete vocal score,[11] and a reading of it shows it to be not only ingenious but also true to the essence of Stein's plotless play. This leads us to realize that, in creating linguistic analogues of her saints, Stein has been able to render their essential natures and that what happens on the stage is quite unimportant as long as the action that a director or scenarist evolves is somehow "true" to the essence of the characters and their landscape. Given the extreme, almost religious simplicity of Stein's text, a production of *Four Saints* can stand nearly any amount of elaborate, stylized trappings.

In addition, Stein's language is almost perfectly suited to musical adaptation. Thomson himself says it best on the record jacket:

> she loved to write vast finales like Beethoven's great codas, full of emphasis, insistence, and repetition. She wrote poetry, in fact, very much as a composer works. She chose a theme and developed it; or rather, she let the words of it develop themselves through free expansion of sound and sense.
> Putting to music poetry so musically conceived as Gertrude Stein's has long been a pleasure to me. The spontaneity of it, its easy flow, and its deep sincerity have always seemed to me just right for music.

The audience used to opera in foreign languages or willing to accept a work such as Debussy's *Pelléas et Mélisande* that has an almost static plot should have little trouble with *Four Saints*. To surrender one's self to the language and music of this opera is much like looking at a Cubist painting. It is there, demanding not that we make something of it, but only that we allow ourselves to experience it in its totality and its space.

Four Saints is an example of the high point of Stein's middle style. For twenty years after writing *Tender Buttons*, she wrote predominantly Cubist prose and verse in syntactically and logically discontinuous sentences with idiosyncratic new uses for old words and with a contempt for old literary forms and traditions. In the arrogance of her maturity, Stein seemed totally sure of her method, even within such tentative presentations of subject matter as *Four Saints in Three Acts* and as the works in *Geography and Plays*. But in the 1930's, with the approach of old age, Stein's lifelong concern with the problems of identity took on new forms. She wrote *The Autobiography of Alice B. Toklas* in straightforward though idiosyncratic prose, and she achieved a major financial and critical success.

As a celebrity and not just a curiosity, she now felt her identity threatened; and some of these psychological problems need to be discussed in connection with *The Autobiography of Alice B. Toklas* and *Everybody's Autobiography* and with such works as *The Geographical History of America*. The crucial matter that concerns us now is the fact that both the kinds of things Stein was writing as well as her way of writing them changed quite radically after the successes of *The Autobiography of Alice B. Toklas* and *Four Saints*.

<h3 style="text-align:center">V　Doctor Faustus Lights the Lights</h3>

Doctor Faustus Lights the Lights is quite representative of Stein's work in the 1930's. In this play she uses a continuous plot, something she had almost totally abandoned since *The Making of Americans*. The syntax is also continuous, and the speakers respond directly to one another. While the style is still flat, repetitive, ritualistic, and full of internal as well as end rhymes, it does "make sense"; and it contains a sufficient number of semantic ambiguities to enable the critic to talk once more about things like metaphor, symbolism, and theme. *Doctor Faustus* is still very recognizably a work of Gertrude Stein's, but it is also part of a literary tradition external to its author.

Stein's Faust is an American version of the Renaissance figure. He has invented the electric light; but, being surrounded at the opera's opening by somewhat dim light bulbs, he finds himself bored by them and begins to question whether he should have sold his soul to the devil or whether he even has had a soul to sell. The question of his own identity is uppermost in Faust's mind. The story contains some traditional characters from the Faust legend: Mephisto and, reflecting both Goethe and Marlowe, a girl with the compound name of "Marguerite Ida and Helena Annabel." The girl has been bitten by a viper; and, although Faust does not seem able to see her, he finally saves her through a form of hypnosis. She then enters into a life of devotion, holding by her side an artificial viper. At one point, she is almost tempted away by a "man from over the seas" before Mephisto stops him. When Faustus (he is alternately called Faustus, Doctor Faustus, and Faust) hears the girl's claim that she can turn night into day, he admits that he is not the only inventor — even though he has previously claimed such exclusive preeminence as inventor of the electric light.

A boy and a talking dog play major symbolic roles in the opera. Faust, who is bored by his present identity, now wishes to go to hell. Mephisto advises him to commit a sin; and, following this advice,

Faust kills the boy and the dog with the help of a real serpent. Mephisto suggests that Faust make himself young again and take Marguerite Ida and Helena Annabel with him to hell. When Faust attempts to do so, the girl rejects him and faints. The lights by this time are darkened; and, at the end, while the man from the seas is holding the girl, Mephisto spirits Faustus down to hell.

Doctor Faustus was written as an opera, complete with ballets, like Gounod's version of the Faust story. Stein expected Lord Gerald Berners to write the score for her, but he was unable to do that kind of work at the end of the 1930s, and the libretto was not even published for another decade. According to Richard Bridgman, "Doctor Faustus was produced as a play in 1951 at the Cherry Lane Theater in New York, with incidental music by Richard Banks" (289n). Although it is one of Stein's most interesting compositions, it has not until recently received much critical attention.

In Gertrude Stein and the Present, however, Allegra Stewart has suggested a lengthy and ingenious Jungian interpretation of Doctor Faustus.[12] She sees in the story the process of Faustus's "individuation," and she invokes all of Jung's categories to support her interpretation, which seems a bit tenuous in many particulars; but the interested reader ought to examine it. What we can agree with, however, is Miss Stewart's contention that this drama is concerned basically with the problems of identity and being — lifelong concerns that, as has been suggested, became even more crucial for Stein during these years. The realization of success is as empty for Faustus as is the emptiness of his invention itself. The illumination to be gotten from the electric lights is minimal or nonexistent. In fact, the darkness of hell seems quite inviting to Faustus, although he finally discovers that he can go there only on Mephisto's, and not on his own, terms.

Stein was not a conventionally reverent person. Still, her concerns are often similar to those of such religiously oriented writers as T. S. Eliot. She too was interested in sainthood and contemplation, not just as religious problems, but as problems of identity. What did it mean to discover one's own essence, in the manner of a traditional saint? And having discovered it, what can one do with it? Faust, though not a saint, does little with his essential knowledge; and he seems, unlike Stein's putative saints, never to have found either ease or peace within his own psyche. He is a tormented modern figure who even wishes to go to hell by himself and yet is thwarted by being carried there by someone who violates him. But Faust has chosen his own violation many times, and he has come to realize that, even though a man must basically live alone inside his own head, his life and even his death must occur in relation to other people. His great discovery of the electric bulb finally gives no light at all and, in the end, darkness covers everything. Faustus is unhappy, and the audience is offered no enlightenment. At the end of the 1930s, the clouds of Hitler's Reich were darkening Europe; and, even though Stein has often been accused of being thoroughly apolitical, she nonetheless felt darkness at that point to be the lot of Western man.

In this regard, we must agree with Richard Bridgman's negative judgment of Stewart's contention that, at the end of the opera, Faustus's tripartite psyche has come into "healthy balance." We find Stein's usual ebullience not terribly positive in 1938, and her sense of the human prospect is not exactly optimistic. She was a more sensitive barometer of her time than many people have cared to admit. That she then felt her sense of self threatened only strengthens the intensity with which we are made to feel Faustus's and — because he is made to represent the rest of us — Western man's decline into the dark abyss that unmistakably began to occur a year later.

It should be quite apparent that the terms with which we are able to discuss this play are markedly different from those we have been able to use for quite a while in discussing Stein's work. By this time in her career, Stein is no longer interested in proving that works of art, like language, can be discussed purely in terms of structure and syntax. Her language now focuses on something other than its own structure; she shifts its concerns to such traditional literary problems as those of moral value and human identity; but she still maintains throughout the play a style readily identifiable as her own.

Stein's interest in dramatic forms continued to evolve as she continued to work in her later style. The next form she tried was the melodrama, a mode she had discussed in her lecture on "Plays" in *Lectures in America*. Here, as everywhere else, Stein's conception of melodrama is uniquely her own. She tried the form in a few shorter pieces that are similar to *Doctor Faustus* in their general adherence to the traditions of dramatic continuity and psychology, but they are nonetheless distinguished by the cleverness of Stein's language. For instance, there is the short play, "Three Sisters Who Were Not Sisters,"[13] in which cleverness goes beyond the mere child's wit of the title. In this melodrama, which is about five people who decide to make up and then enact a murder mystery, no one is ever aware of who among them is either the victim or the murderer until the lights come on and the scene is over. Stein was a lover of mystery stories, and even wrote about why she loved them.[14] But she was also a marvelous observer of how human beings interact in particular situations, and even in the plays that are tedious — and most of them are — she nonetheless usually conveys a clear, hard psychological sense of the basic personalities and "sounds" coming out of her characters. Stein was never a master of dramatic movement and plot, but to the reader — we are never quite confident that most of the plays will work well on the stage, although some of them have had successful productions — there is always a steady fascination in the "story," and quite often a strikingly sudden emotion is evoked by a scene or a speech.

VI   Yes Is For a Very Young Man

The first of Stein's nonmusical plays to be produced was a play about the French Resistance, *Yes Is For a Very Young Man,* originally published as *In Savoy,* which played in Pasadena, California, just a few months before Stein's death.[15] The performance seems to have been well received there and in its few public performances after that. However, the reader can recognize a number of problems with it as a play, not the least of which is its talkiness.

The young man of the title is Ferdinand, a young Frenchman who in the first act pays court on Constance, an American woman living in France during the Occupation (much like Gertrude Stein). Ferdinand is sensitive to all the positions possible for a Frenchman at this time. He is not partisan enough to become a *maquis* in the Resistance, but he is too much a patriot simply to collaborate with the Pétain regime. When he is ordered to Germany to work in a factory, he refuses. But he has brothers there, and he does not wish reprisals taken against them; so he goes to Germany, where he becomes foreman of the factory and representative of the French workers to the Germans. After returning mysteriously to France for the Liberation, he returns to Germany to lead the resistance there.

By contrast, Ferdinand's brother Henry is a hotheaded French patriot who is married to a very conservative woman, Denise, whose brother Achile has joined Pétain. It is clear, however, that Achile is motivated as much by adventure as by expedience; for, before joining the Vichy army, he had shot down half a dozen Nazi planes; and, after the Liberation, he wants to go to the Pacific to fight the Japanese. But Henry sees only expediency in Achile's behavior; and, when Henry joins the Resistance himself, he is aided in this effort by Ferdinand's American friend Constance. The situation is not all black and white, however, for Stein shows how strongly Henry still feels toward his wife and child and how his conflicting loyalties are ultimately more basic to his humanity than any kind of patriotic emotion.

In a play with a heavy emotional content, a static plot is usually a serious liability, especially since this play, unlike Stein's operas, did not have the help of Virgil Thomson's music. Still, even though Richard Bridgman has cast his vote against it, I find *Yes* to be an often charming and even quite moving piece of drama. It begins slowly with a lot of repetitive, circular speeches that are full of the topics of ordinary domesticity but that lack much of the tension to be expected in a group of people trapped by the German occupation of France. But, as is so often the case, Stein is only warming up. After she has established who her characters are and how they are to interact, we begin to get quite caught up in their personal dramas.

Like her mentor Henry James, whose experience as a dramatist was also somewhat equivocal, Stein is at her best in dealing with how people behave in situations, particularly difficult ones. She knows how they interact; how they respond in crises. And she does not get trapped into painting her characters with moral shadings. In *Yes*, her so-called political naiveté worked to her artistic advantage, for this drama is not a fanatically partisan work like so many of the war movies and plays of the time. Although some of her friends, such as Bernard Faÿ, were later branded as *collaborateurs*, Stein remained on the political sidelines in *Yes;* and her emotional stolidity kept her nonpartisan until well toward the end of the German occupation. To understand this aspect of the play, the reader should read it concurrently with *Wars I Have Seen*, Stein's memoir-diary of her experiences as an exile in a French village during World War II. This book makes it clear that Stein was less interested in taking sides than she was in examining what little things people will do to survive during difficult times and in challenging situations.

After Stein seems sure of her characters and how they interact, her dialogue becomes more deft and her handling of dramatic incident more confident. Because *Yes* is a conventionally plotted play, we feel more annoyed with Stein's lack of concision than we normally would; but, had the play had the benefit of a New York production, it would surely have been pruned to the more satisfactory shape of the well-made play. Without apologies, however, *Yes Is For a Very*

Young Man shows most of Stein's virtues as a dramatist, especially her sense of basic social realities and of the complexity of interpersonal relationships. While *Yes* is not simply a "happy" play, the serenity that is its overall mood is clearly congruent with other works of the same period such as *Wars I Have Seen, Paris France,* and *Brewsie and Willie.* With only a few years left to live, Stein was definitely entering a valedictory stage. Her final works are among her calmest and most accepting.

VII The Mother of Us All

Very much at one with the mood of these years is Stein's last full-length work, *The Mother of Us All,* an opera based loosely on the life of Susan B. Anthony and scored once again by Virgil Thomson. The first performance of this piece took place almost a year after Stein's death by cancer in July 1946, and was memorialized by a sumptuous edition of the score that includes Maurice Grosser's scenario and photographs of Stein and Thomson by Carl Van Vechten.[16] For me, *The Mother of Us All* is Stein's finest contribution to stage literature and is also one of the major works of her late period. Of the other plays considered in this chapter, it is most like *Doctor Faustus Lights the Lights;* but its language is more controlled, and its staging is theatrically imaginative. In remarks prefatory to the scenario, Maurice Grosser describes *The Mother of Us All* as "a pageant," and the play's formal fluidity makes that description quite apt. Many American readers will remember the pageants in which they were compelled to act during junior high school days, dramatic events usually seasoned with a heavy dose of patriotism; and one side of Stein revelled in this kind of Americana. The mother of Modernism could also create dramas with the period flavor of a Brady daguerrotype or a Currier and Ives lithograph.

The cast of characters in *The Mother of Us All* consists of not only Susan B. Anthony and her companion Anne, but also of American figures ranging from John Adams, Daniel Webster, Andrew Johnson, and Ulysses Grant, to Lillian Russell, and then to "Gertrude S." and her contemporaries. Among her own friends Stein includes by name "Virgil T.," Donald Gallup, and Constance Fletcher. This kind of ahistoricity abounds in the conventional pageant, and it should give the reader no trouble. As Maurice Grosser suggests, such "a spectacle [is] no more anachronistic than that suggested to the mind by the perusal of a volume of old photographs" (13). Stein's point in this opera has little to do with history, American or otherwise, except in the way history can be made to buttress her assessment of herself.

To summarize the plot of *The Mother of Us All* succinctly is not really possible, for Stein makes full use of the generic fluidity of the pageant. Many of the characters in the play are figures from the mid-nineteenth century, but because Stein clearly feels no obligation to be historical she does not use the events of the time to provide more than the loosest kind of continuous structure to the events in the opera. The characters most often function as symbolic counters to one another, particularly in the contrasts Stein poses between Susan B. Anthony, Lillian Russell, Daniel Webster, Anthony Comstock, and Ulysses Grant. Set speeches abound in the arias, and what supplies the driving force behind the stage happenings is the way that Stein uses the characters, events, and ideas of her opera to act out her own evaluation at the end of her life of what her career has meant.

In this regard, it is clear that she identifies with Susan B. Anthony, but not because Stein was much concerned with the problems of female equality or suffrage. She did not march in parades for Women's Right to Vote, although she did go to medical school in the 1890s and later opted for a life in which she exercised her own choices free from the dominance of men (after the early years with Leo in Paris). No one has ever accused her of subservience. But she was in many ways like the historical Susan B. Anthony because of her lonely struggle for the victory of Modernism in literature and painting. Miss Anthony died in 1906, fully fourteen years before her efforts resulted in the Nineteenth Amendment; and she was ridiculed throughout her life, by women as well as by men, and was considered both a crank and a nuisance.

Stein also saw herself as a crusader, increasingly so until the early 1930s when she experienced her first great popular successes. She too was ridiculed; and, among those who claimed to take "art" seriously, she was often regarded as a menace. Even her successes did not bring with them any lasting inner peace, although they were often a source of satisfaction. For a woman who was used to aligning herself against the forces of "mammon," her new financial ease and public recognition brought a great deal of self-doubt. She could never be sure she was being taken seriously or was just being patronized as the clown princess of modern art. As a result, she must have shared many of the feelings she projected as those of Susan B. Anthony. Feeling the abdominal pains symptomatic of her fatal cancer, Stein must have been tempted to wonder even more seriously about whether her life had meant anything.

Still, we must take issue with Richard Bridgman who finds *The Mother of Us All* to be one of Stein's most bitter works. Granted, she ventilates previously suppressed feelings about men that she had begun to release in *Brewsie and Willie*, feelings that Bridgman traces back to unresolved problems with her father, Daniel Stein (342). The words Susan Anthony uses to describe men are often explicitly vituperative, and the men in the play are, by and large, portrayed unflatteringly. Still, the interchanges are both high-spirited and thoughtful. *The Mother of Us All* is decidedly not just a polemic against either men or the ugly forces of life. That Stein seems finally to see herself as a martyr for the cause of Modernism does not change the fact that she has portrayed her characters with a gusto uncommon in a writer approaching the end of a long lifetime. The facts of this vitality, inventiveness, and good-humored wit, when combined with the charm of Stein's use of history and contemplation, make this work a remarkable performance.

" 'My long life, my long life,' " Susan Anthony concludes in the last line of the play as her monument is being unveiled.[17] This statement is not just "the bleak sum of mother's wisdom," as Richard Bridgman has suggested (345). The tone is as much one of acceptance as one of despair, a positive though quietly contemplative affirmation of having lived and struggled. As the vehicle of such emotions, *The Mother of Us All* is unusual in the Stein canon, although the work of her final decade did move in the direction of greater emotional openness.

CHAPTER 6

Novels

F OR someone who began her career as a novelist and is
still associated in the public's mind primarily with the writing of
novels and memoirs, Gertrude Stein wrote surprisingly few full-
length works of fiction after the prolific period of *The Making of
Americans, Two,* and *A Long Gay Book.* For more than a decade she
produced hermetic, experimental works, very few of which were of a
sustained length and all of which derived their styles from her
previous experiments in portraiture and still lifes. The first book-
length work not simply a collection of shorter pieces that Stein wrote
after 1912 was *A Novel of Thank You,* which was begun in 1925.
After that, she produced only half a dozen long works that we could
consider novels; for one of them, *The World Is Round,* is a book for
children.

As usual, Stein's handling of a traditional literary form raises basic
questions about the genre. Even during decades in which the word
"plot" had become taboo, Stein uses less plot than any novelist of
her era. She writes books with no dramatic development — books in
which one event follows another in much the same way that events
follow one another in everyday life. Even more, she creates works in
which her characters simply inhabit a verbal landscape and do
nothing at all.

The novels, like the plays of this period, exemplify the shifts from
the middle to the later phase of Stein's development. *A Novel of
Thank You* (1925) and *Lucy Church Amiably* (1927) are written
primarily in the hermetic style to which we are accustomed. But in
the detective story, *Blood on the Dining-Room Floor* (1933), and
later in her children's novel, *The World Is Round* (1938), we see a
transition into greater continuity and communicability that is continued with many variations through *Ida, A Novel* (1940), *Mrs.
Reynolds* (1940 - 1942), and *Brewsie and Willie* (1945). Within this

larger context of stylistic continuity, however, Stein tackles different problems in every one of her works; but she maintains the attitude she shared with other Modernist artists of seeing each new phase of her work as posing problems to be solved — and of feeling the constant necessity to "make it new." In the course of this attempt, Stein wrote a few novels that deserve to be considered among her most impressive achievements.

I A Novel of Thank You

Although it remained unpublished until 1958, *A Novel of Thank You* was written during 1925 and 1926, a period Carl Van Vechten has described as being "not very prolific years for our author."[1] According to Van Vechten, Stein had decided "to write in a more obscure vein than she had employed hitherto in her career" (ix); and the book she actually produced more than adequately fulfills that expectation. I can think of no work of Stein's that the unaccustomed reader is more likely to read with such total incomprehension, and to call it a novel is to redefine our conception of that genre. While *A Novel of Thank You* does have a kind of a buried narrative that Richard Bridgman locates in Stein's relationship with Alice Toklas,[2] that story is almost impossible for us to follow; and I shall not even attempt to summarize its "plot." What the book seems most like is a hermetic diary-commonplace book. Stein includes the names of many of her friends, much in the manner of *A Long Gay Book;* and, in Van Vechten's "Introduction" to *A Novel of Thank You*, he lists Alice Toklas's identifications of these people. In some ways this work is the most personal longer one that Stein wrote, although the story's emotional effect is controlled, as usual, through the abstractness of the narrative presentation.

The book consists largely of remembered conversations and short experiences, and the contents have little narrative continuity or story line. It is as though Stein recorded every night the few new things that had happened to her during the day or listed what she might have remembered from the past. The styles used are largely those developed in the portraits and in *Tender Buttons,* styles she repeated and refined during her middle period. There are occasional reflections on the nature of fiction: "What is a surprise. A continued story is a surprise. This is a continued story, this is a surprise this is a continued story. What is a surprise, a continued story is a surprise. This is a continued story, a surprise a continued story is a surprise" (13). But such remarks in their fictional context often have the ring of a rationalization. Stein uses her narrator the way she has ever since *The Making of Americans* — to comment on the action and to speak in the author's voice as she records the immediate thoughts and directions that emanate from her consciousness. The chapters are all very short and are often numbered eccentrically; for instance, part 1 of the novel contains 316 such chapters in 237 pages; part 2, which is a little over a page, has three chapters; and part 3 contains one two-page chapter. As usual, Stein is telling us with such idiosyncrasies that numerical divisions in longer works of literature are both arbitrary and meaningless.

The language is full of puns ("Minnie Singer" [32]), clichés ("Hanging fire" [48]), familiar definitions ("Action and reaction are equal and opposite." [32]), and phrases that sound like conventional apothegms but are coinages of Stein's ("A novel of thank you is historic." [198]). The reason for this *mélange* of linguistic game-playing is that the tone of *A Novel of Thank You* is primarily that of dialogue, spoken, overheard, remembered, familiar. This tone takes over almost completely in the last third of the book where the more formal tone disappears. Also in this section the book's main repetitive motif takes over, that of "Thank you." This phrase is repeated again and again in many contexts and phrasings. It is almost as though the purpose of the book is to define its title by incantation. Stein also uses for the first time one of her more famous phrases: "Before the flowers of friendship faded friendship faded" (43).

Even though the chapters from the middle of the book onward often seem to describe self-contained episodes abstractly, there is little continuity short of the verbal contents of Stein's consciousness as they are spilled onto the page. To the student of Stein, the contents of her consciousness might be quite interesting; but, to the less committed reader, *A Novel of Thank You* has very little to offer. It is important to us because it marks Stein's return to the longer forms of prose with which she began her career and in which she was to work intermittently from the middle 1920s on.

II Lucy Church Amiably

Stein's next full-length "novel" *Lucy Church Amiably* is a "landscape" very much in the mode of *Four Saints in Three Acts* which was written at the same time. A "pastoral," *Lucy Church Amiably* is surely one of the gentlest works Stein ever wrote, as well as one of her most difficult. On the title page, Stein appended the following description: "A Novel of Romantic beauty and nature and which Looks Like an Engraving."[3] A further indication of the book's elegiac tone is given by its epigraph: "And with a nod she turned her head toward the falling water. Amiably." The language of *Lucy Church* is as unstrained as the simplest kinds of thoughts a saint might have while experiencing enlightenment or a union with God and nature. In this regard, the work is much like Stein's other writings about saints; and her identification with the Lucy Church of the title shows her basic religious orientation.

Lucy Church Amiably, while it is a full-length work of prose fiction, is not really a novel; it is an extended meditation on the meaning of a particular place, which is why Gertrude Stein described it as a "landscape." Although there is a series of characters, none is given more flesh in the book than a mere name. A number of localities in that part of provincial France are mentioned, as are many of the plants grown in the area; but none of these adds up to a continuous narrative. *Lucy Church Amiably* is more like an extended prose poem; or, as Richard Bridgman has best described it, "The book is essentially a long, lyric diary, begun in May, lackadaisical as a vacation, and little more than what she herself called it, a landscape . . . in which there are some people" (190).

The landscape qualities of this book, its position as one of Stein's full-length "geographies," become apparent with even a cursory reading. The title character is named after a "little church with a pagoda-like steeple at Lucey in the region of Belley,"[4] an area where Stein and Alice Toklas had a summer home for many years. Local characters figure prominently in the narrative as does the region's vegetation and topography. The strong sense of place is aided by what John Malcolm Brinnin describes as "an increased melodiousness in the line-to-line composition of the language" (294). We feel, often without knowing why, what it must be like to be in that particular spot or even, in fact, to *be* that particular spot. In that sense, *Lucy Church Amiably* is in strong contrast to *A Novel of Thank You* in which we have no real sense of place but know somehow what it is like to be inside the head of characters, hearing what they say, think, remember.

Lucy Church also has a greater sense of novelistic continuity than its predecessor. It is concerned, at least nominally, with the same set of characters all the way through; and its chapters have a relatively standard length (around fifteen pages) throughout the first three-quarters of the book. Toward the end, as is often the case, Stein seems to have lost some of her vital interest in the project; and the chapters often dwindle to only a page or two, and occasionally to just three or four lines. The characters most continually in evidence are Lucy Church, Simon Therese, John Mary, Albert Bigelow, and Lilian Ann St. Peter Stanhope. Many of them obviously bear the names of both sexes, a phenomenon that not only reveals the author's sexual ambivalence but, more important, creates for the reader a sense of the asexual quality of the saintly or the ideally religious. Surely a saint is someone beyond the potential torments of sexuality, whether epicene, like a Della Robia figure of Christ, or serene, like a meditative Boddhisattva.

The continuities of fictional narrative are limited in *Lucy Church*, however, even with the book's continued focus on the same named people and its continuous reference to the setting of the church and to the vegetational topography. For, once again, there is no really discernible plot here. If this "novel" were one of Stein's "plays," it could be used by a scenarist like Maurice Grosser just as open-endedly as was the text of *Four Saints*. Stein does not return to chronological continuity until *The Autobiography of Alice B. Toklas*.

The few critical estimates of *Lucy Church Amiably* range from Donald Sutherland's judgment of it as "the purest and best pastoral romance we have had in this century"[5] to Richard Bridgman's description of its prose as "banal" and "lackadaisical" (190). Sutherland's judgment is a lefthanded compliment since the pastoral romance scarcely exists in our time, and Bridgman's judgment could just as easily have called the language "simple" and "unhurried." *Lucy Church* can be characterized as a lyrical, easygoing work that depends on the usual Stein word play, including rhymes, puns, and the author's incurably pseudo-aphoristic style. What is striking, however, especially after *A Novel of Thank You*, is the way *Lucy Church* seems to verge on comprehensibility.

While its plot is almost nonexistent and while its characters are little more than names, the book has a genuine continuity of theme and of phrase as well as a style of elegant grammatical linkage. The words seem ready to be explicit on almost every occasion. *A Novel of Thank You* makes no pretense about its hermeticism, and we immediately feel in reading it that comprehensibility is a false expectation, but with *Lucy Church* we constantly expect meaning to emerge. Richard Bridgman has noted that in the late 1920s Stein was already beginning to feel the need to explain herself. She had given the lecture "Composition as Explanation" at Oxford (1926) and was getting involved in the public performance of her works in the theater. It is clear that she was becoming increasingly aware of the presence of an audience. In addition, Stein and Alice Toklas were planning to publish all of Stein's manuscripts in the Plain Edition, of which *Lucy Church Amiably* was the first to appear. *The Autobiography of Alice B. Toklas* was only half a decade away.

III   Blood on the Dining-Room Floor

Stein's lifelong interest in detective stories and her concern during this time over her threatened sense of identity led to her next "novel," a detective story with the marvelously melodramatic title, *Blood on the Dining-Room Floor* (1933).[6] The story, whose melodrama ends with its title, arose from an incident that occurred at a hotel in Belley where Stein and Alice Toklas had taken summer vacations for the past seven years. One day the manager's wife, a Madame Pernollet, fell out of one of the hotel windows onto the courtyard; and her body was removed so quickly that the hotel guests did not even know what happened. For the bourgeois mind so dear to Stein, particularly that of the French bourgeoisie, sentiment must never interfere with business. The dead are dead. Stein was quite fascinated by how the mystery of whether the lady's death was accidental, suicidal, or homicidal was never solved nor even seriously investigated.

As we might imagine, *Blood on the Dining-Room Floor* is a mystery story without any genuine sense of mystery; and, since the mystery was never solved about the real-life counterpart, Stein's fictional version has no solution. But, by the end, the reader does not care; we have been privy to an extended Stein meditation about French provincial families and about the way a violent death can have consequences for them, especially when the people who know about it are discreet. The story is only eight pages long, but it has twenty chapters. Since the first one has twenty pages, it is apparent that Stein, as usual, lost interest in her project and sustained her energies through fragmentation.

The style of *Blood on the Dining-Room Floor* is comprehensible and informal; it echoes the rhythms of speech and contains the usual directions from the author to herself and her readers. The sentences are short, noncinematic, and only occasionally lyrical or poetic. The major reader interest is not linguistic but generic; it lies in watching Stein take a traditional, ritualistic form like the detective story and violate almost all of its conventions while still maintaining somehow the basic tone and concerns familiar to it. Although *Blood on the Dining-Room Floor* is like no other detective story, it quite definitely falls within that genre, and it points out by its irreverence the artificiality of many of the "whodunit's" conventional concerns.

IV The World Is Round

Except for a few shorter works of fiction, some of which were published in the Yale Edition volumes *As Fine as Melanctha* and *Mrs. Reynolds and Earlier Novelettes,* Stein's next full-length narrative was the children's novel *The World Is Round.* This short book should be read within the context of Stein's contemplations of identity, human nature, and human mind, such as *The Geographical History of America* and *Four in America.* Both the children about whom the book is written, a little girl named Rose and her cousin Willie, are extremely conscious of who they are and what relation their names have to their sense of themselves. It is doubly interesting to consider that the girl's name is Rose and that Stein's most famous line, "A rose is a rose is a rose" (only three roses this time), appears as the book's motto above the dedication in a circle strongly suggestive of a mandala. It is no coincidence that Stein was heavily concerned with the threat to her identity caused by her becoming a celebrity and that a similar device appeared at the top of Stein's personal stationery. Little Rose is both fascinated and disturbed by the fact that the world is round, that one can walk round and round on it, much, as Richard Bridgman suggests (300), like the serpent of the uroboric circle who has his tail in his mouth. The connection between this concern and the mandala of roses is obvious. As Erich Neumann has indicated, such concerns in primitive cultures have much to do with the process of individuation.[7] In a Modernist primitive, they no doubt have much to do with the same process. Bridgman gives a good capsule summary of the plot of *The World Is Round:*

Rose is a rather willful, disturbed girl who . . . questions for herself who she is. Particularly depressed to discover that everything goes round, when she sings, she cries. Her cousin Willie is an adventurous boy who becomes excited when he sings. At the conclusion of their adventures, they are revealed to be unrelated, which permits them to marry, have children, and live happily ever after. But before that traditional close, they undergo several enigmatic experiences, the first involving a lion, the second, the climbing of a mountain. The conquering of fears, self-exploration, aspiration, and success are all components of the story. (299 - 300)

The story is composed of a series of readily understandable episodes concerning the adventures, more psychological than is usual in children's books, of Rose and Willie. What I wish to suggest is that this is one of Stein's most successful works, particularly in its unification of style and subject. Like Matisse who wished to paint with the eyes of a child, Stein combines primitivistically simple diction with interlocking repetitions, as well as a humorous tone that mixes the pretense of seriousness with the fun of writing.[8]

This combination works admirably in conveying the consciousness of a child as she tries to locate a place for herself within the world. For a woman who never had children of her own, Stein seems remarkably in touch with a child's mind, perhaps because in one side of her personality she kept the child in herself very active. And, from personal experience, I can attest that children find the book delightful. It is warm and serious, funny and sad; it is consistent with Stein's basic concerns about the nature of personality and identity; and it is very much in the direct line of her stylistic development. No one, even though it is clearly a tale for children written in an easily understandable style and containing a recognizable story, could mistake the author of this book.

V   Ida, A Novel

Written in a more serious vein, although still full of fun, *Ida, A Novel*, was written in 1940 and published by Random House the following year.[9] It reminds me at least of the shorter tales in *Three Lives* ("The Good Anna" and "The Gentle Lena") because of the stylized discontinuities of its prose and its mock-gentle treatment of the heroine. This novel, however, is much more difficult than the earlier stories because more than thirty years of Stein's mature abstractionism have molded its style.

Supposedly based, at least initially, on the life of Wallis Warfield Simpson, the Baltimore divorcee who had recently married King Edward, the final version of *Ida* has little to do with the Duchess of Windsor. It is, as Donald Sutherland has suggested, "the story of what Gertrude Stein called a 'publicity saint,' that is a person who neither does anything nor is connected with anything but who by sheer force of existence in being there holds the public attention and becomes a legend" (154). As was common in the works Stein wrote after *The Autobiography of Alice B. Toklas*, the main emphasis in *Ida* is on the problem of identity — and most particularly that of the author. As Sutherland also says, "Ida is a sort of combination of

Helen of Troy, Dulcinea, Garbo, the Duchess of Windsor, and in particular 'Gertrude Stein.' " The last named is in quotation marks because it is the image of herself in publicity that was at this time most threatening to Stein's sense of herself. The material of *Ida* draws on incidents from Stein's own past, some from as far back as her childhood, that were first mentioned in themes she wrote at Radcliffe; she also fills the book with a lot of her negative feelings about men. The specific allusions to the Duchess of Windsor that remain seem limited to the fact that Ida is married and divorced a number of times.

To all the bizarre incidents that occur in her life, Ida reacts with little emotion. She merely questions occasionally what everything means in relation to her sense of self. Like Joyce's Stephen Dedalus who wishes to be his own father, Ida tries to control her own identity to the point of wishing herself a twin sister. We are told at the beginning that Ida did indeed have a twin, Ida-Ida; but we see nothing of this second self until Ida herself is eighteen, at which time she decides how pleasant it would be to have a twin. In singing to one of her many dogs, Ida says: "Oh dear oh dear Love, that was her dog, if I had a twin well nobody would know which one I was and which one she was and so if anything happened nobody could tell anything and lots of things are going to happen and oh Love I felt it yes I know it I have a twin" (11).

When Ida wins a beauty contest, the twin becomes a major factor in her life because she now has a "publicity" half; and, in order to combat the threat to her identity, she names her twin "Winnie" because she is always winning. She uses her twin basically as an object on which to project her alienated self; but after a time Winnie disappears, and, as Bridgman suggests, the novel becomes "tedious" (308). Sutherland proposes that *Ida* is an existentialist novel whose main character is more "contingent" than any in Franz Kafka. "Much of the book," he says, "is an account of her search for her essence, for self-realization" (157). Because of the way in which Ida adjusts to all situations without feeling her personality destroyed, she ironically represents Gertrude Stein's concept of the "human mind." She has, in fact, no personality; and, as Stein claimed in *The Geographical History of America*, personality has nothing to do with the human mind; it is a manifestation of human nature.

Ida is composed of a series of incidents that do not develop into a plot. These incidents function primarily as a set of examples of how publicity can create an identity that has nothing to do with per-

sonality and yet also has nothing positive to offer in the way of a
sense of self to the main character, the author, or the reader. *Ida* is a
bleak novel in this regard; it is more specifically autobiographical
than any plotted work of fiction Stein had written in thirty years, but
it contains just as dark a view of humanity as any of her early books.
And yet, the bleakness of Stein's ultimate vision is counterbalanced
by some of the most humorous writing she has done, at least in the
lighter sections early in the book. It is too much to claim *Ida* to be an
existentialialist masterpiece, but the book is in many ways one of the
more successful productions of Stein's later years. However, it is not
so fine a work as *Mrs. Reynolds*, Stein's first fictional response to
World War II.

VI   Mrs. Reynolds

Mrs. Reynolds[10] is the longest work of fiction Stein composed after
The Making of Americans; and, while it is not so difficult as some
pieces of Stein's middle period, it is written in a much more difficult
and discontinuous style than was *Ida* just a year earlier. Although the
setting of *Mrs. Reynolds* is never really specified, Richard Bridgman
is right in suggesting that the novel takes place in occupied France.
The characters have English names, as do the two centrally evil
presences in the book, Angel Harper — meant to be Adolph Hitler
— and Joseph Lane — supposed to represent Joseph Stalin.

Although we never get to meet either of the evil men, they are
major figures in the novel, particularly Angel Harper, whose increasing age as the book goes on is meant to represent the growing
menace of Nazi Germany and the continued ascendancy of the
troubled dictator. Juxtaposed against the quiet domesticity of Mr.
and Mrs. Reynolds are quick flashes into the mind of Angel Harper
as he remembers his life, particularly during his adolescence. As
Harper grows older, Mrs. Reynolds in her seemingly endless conversations becomes more and more disturbed at his increasing age.
By contrast, Joseph Lane diminishes rapidly; and, by the end, he is
merely an occasional name. But the sense of fear and helplessness
conveyed through juxtaposing the simple Mrs. Reynolds (we never
learn her first name) and the evil Angel Harper gives us an effective
sense of how many people felt as they watched with unbelieving
eyes the accession to power of the obviously demented German
Führer. In her flashbacks to Harper's youth, Stein manages to convey the sense of a disturbed childhood, the kind of background that
would adequately have given rise to the kind of madness Hitler often

displayed. And yet the portrait of Harper is not drawn without sympathy. He is a complex person, not merely a figure from nineteenth-century melodrama; and the fact of his psychic complexity, when combined with the terror of Mrs. Reynolds, has a subtle but powerful effect on the reader.

The echoes of Gertrude Stein that appear in Mrs. Reynolds make it clear that this is a personal book. As Bridgman says, "Mrs. Reynolds is not altogether an autobiographical figure, even though she is 'heavy' and 'quite plump,' has dogs, meditates on George Washington, reads detective stories, takes walks, gardens, talks with the neighbors, and generally engages in those activities that Alice Toklas and Gertrude Stein did when they were in the country, including contemplating flight, then deciding against it. . . . Mr. and Mrs. Reynolds seem to be composites of Gertrude Stein and Alice Toklas" (320).

Stein herself spent the war in the French provinces, tending her garden, thinking her thoughts, writing *Wars I Have Seen*, and feeling confused about how the solid middle-class world she treasured so much had broken down. The quiet heroism of her own wartime endurance is mirrored in Mrs. Reynolds, just as Stein's sense of the continuity of ordinary life throughout all the vicissitudes of a world war is mirrored in the fact that life goes on as usual in the little village where the Reynoldses live with "the oppressive cloud of Angel Harper" hanging over all.

In a short epilogue to the book, Stein clarifies her intentions: "This book is an effort to show the way anybody could feel these years. It is a perfectly ordinary couple living an ordinary life and having ordinary conversations and really not suffering personally from everything that is happening but over them, all over them is the shadow of two men, and then the shadow of one of the two men gets bigger and then blows away and there is no other. There is nothing historical about this book except the state of mind" (267). Stein is toughminded and persistent in following the simplicity of her vision, and the reader is left with an overwhelming sense of the "state of mind" that she has wished to convey — that of an ordinary life of quiet desperation lived without undue consternation but on a continuous level of terror.

The reader who tries to get through *Mrs. Reynolds* in a few long sittings the way he would an ordinary novel is making a mistake, for Stein includes as usual in her narrative a continuous repetition of daily events that only bore someone who is waiting for events to "happen." But the reader who limits himself to thirty or forty pages at a sitting will find that he has read one of the most disturbing books to have come out of the war. Although Stein's novel is rarely discussed, *Mrs. Reynolds* is surely her finest one since *The Making of Americans*.

VII   Brewsie and Willie

Not so much can be said, however, for the last full-length work of fiction that Stein wrote, *Brewsie and Willie*,[11] although in a more limited way it is still a successful performance. The book is a record of the extreme partisanship Stein developed for the American soldiers who came into France with the army of liberation. Primarily a series of conversations rather than a novel, the chapters of dialogue seem almost to have been recorded by a tape recorder, and they demonstrate the good ear for speech Stein had.

The young foot soldiers of *Brewsie and Willie* talk of world affairs in conversations that reflect their regional backgrounds, their colloquialisms, their arrogance at having conquered the German army. Stein's instinct for slang is usually good, but her use of it in relation to some of the characters is occasionally stilted. Brewsie and Willie are intentionally contrasted according to both their concerns and sensitivities, although they do not disagree on a really fundamental level. Willie is a loudmouth, a blusterer, a stubborn and sarcastic man; Brewsie seems to think more before he speaks and is involved with issues. Although the other characters express many opinions, Brewsie seems to have thought about matters more seriously than anyone else. As the book proceeds, however, Willie undergoes some mellowing.

Richard Bridgman has suggested that Stein found the dialogue form congenial to her in *Brewsie and Willie* because it gave her the opportunity to vent her spleen without obligating her to develop any position logically (336). Stein expresses her hostility toward the American economic system by letting her characters talk about it with contempt and yet by allowing their immaturity to give credence to her feelings that too much prosperity has caused the development of a coddled American male who can not think for himself. The recent Depression is still in the minds of the characters who find much of the evil in America to be symbolized by the Gallup Poll, industrialism, and labor unions.

It is difficult for us today to take Stein's presentation of the issues as seriously as did the early reviewers of *Brewsie and Willie*. Stein has no solutions to suggest, and the dialogue rarely sheds much light on the matters discussed; thus the book is interesting only as a work of fiction. The portraits of "G. I.'s" are among the best we have, but Stein's hostility toward men is obvious throughout the book. Perhaps the most unfortunate thing about *Brewsie and Willie* is the epilogue entitled "To Americans." This peroration on the subject of patriotism that is rampant with unblushing clichés is forgiveable, I suppose, only when we realize that Stein had lived through the occupation of France and had discovered thereby how deeply American she really was.

The conventional novel was never a form in which Stein could work with complete success, however, for her conception of plot and character development was too static. That is why her ritualized pieces, such as "Melanctha," *The Making of Americans, The World Is Round*, and *Mrs. Reynolds* are her best works of fiction; they never lead us to expect anything to "happen." Stein's gift for dialogue, for the evocation of place, and for the rendering of inner psychic realities are most successfully evoked by the incantations of her experimental prose in the novel as well as in the drama. The explanations for her methods are best presented by Stein herself in the series of writings she undertook in the 1920s and continued into the 1930s and 1940s; in them she both explained and demonstrated the rationale behind her peculiar literary techniques — and to these writings we shall now turn.

CHAPTER 7

Theories, Explanations, and Autobiography

AMONG modern literary figures, Gertrude Stein has long been recognized as a great conversationalist. In the beginning, she remained silent while her brother held forth; but, with the advent of Alice Toklas and the final exit of Leo Stein, she emerged as the articulate center of her own circle of painters and writers, many of whom have acknowledged her wisdom about and her insight into the craft of writing. Her influence on Hemingway's style is by this time commonplace knowledge.[1] All those who had the experience of discussing literary matters with her mention in particular her ability to make things thoroughly clear, especially about her own writings; and anyone who has listened to a recording of her reading her own work can only wonder why it is a puzzle to anyone.[2] This phenomenon is due primarily, no doubt, to her marvelous speaking voice and to her powerful personality.

 For most of her life, Stein limited her explanations to the informality of her salon; but, in 1926, with her fame expanding well beyond Paris, she was invited to lecture by the literary societies of both Oxford and Cambridge. The text that emerged, "Composition as Explanation," expounds many ideas central to Stein's thought; but, more important, the preparation of this lecture unlocked a side of Stein that was to become central to her writing. After that lecture, she composed expositions of and meditations about most of her life's passions, such as her theories of grammar, culture, time, identity, painting, narration, detective stories, memory, and money. In the first half of this chapter, we shall consider these philosophical and theoretical meditations, beginning with the well-known and anthologized "Composition as Explanation."[3] Since so much of Stein's crucial thinking is expressed in "Composition as Explanation," we shall not be as detailed in discussing her other short works of criticism. We shall discuss only those that extend the implications of ideas she expressed in this early lecture.

I *"Composition as Explanation"*

The talk "Composition as Explanation," published as it was spoken, is not transparently clear; but it is comprehensible enough even on first reading to make obvious some of the leading ideas in Stein's theories about writing and about the writer's cultural function. To Stein, "There is singularly nothing that makes a difference a difference in beginning and in the middle and in ending except that each generation has something different at which they are all looking."[4] For Stein, a culture is defined by the nature of its perceptions, by the things it chooses to look at; but what the members of a culture see does not control what they do. The perceptual process works in quite the other way, for "what is seen depends upon how everybody is doing everything" (26). The true product of a culture is the kind of consciousness its activities create in the people who live within it. Without entering into the controversy, Stein aligns herself with those who feel that consciousness is created by what the collective individuality *does*. And this collective consciousness is what Stein means when she uses the term "composition." To understand its composition is to be able to explain a culture, and the artist's function is to express the composition of his time. Doing so is an activity he cannot avoid.

"No one is ahead of his time" (27), Stein claims in a statement both insightful and self-justifying. "It is only that the particular variety of creating his time is the one that his contemporaries who also are creating their own time refuse to accept." At this point, Stein begins to develop a theory that has a more complete expression in her essay, "What Are Masterpieces." This theory maintains that the truly creative individual is initially an "outlaw," whose work is considered by his contemporaries as ugly until it is understood; and who, by being understood, becomes classified and thus "classical."

This theory, which she claims to have shared with Picasso, tells us that the critic's task in writing about the works of the past is not to expatiate on their beauties — because beauty is something seen in a work only after it has ceased to shock — but to recapture the "ugliness" in the work — the qualities that made it irritating to the artist's contemporaries. Elements of Stein's need for self-justification creep into her remarks: "If every one were not so indolent they would realize that beauty is beauty even when it is irritating and stimulating not only when it is accepted and classic. Of course it is extremely difficult nothing more so than to remember back to its not being beautiful once it has become beautiful."(29) But the point she makes is valid, notwithstanding the tone of special pleading.

Stein's next major claim is about how things remain the same and yet constantly change, but she is not merely referring to the Heraclitean maxim that one cannot step into the same river twice. Stein asserts not only that physical circumstances remain largely the same in every era, but that human beings share the same emotions no matter when they live. They always feel anger, love, jealousy, and happiness; but what is always different is the "composition" of a particular era. Therefore, "as the composition is different and always going to be different everything is not the same," even though, in the sense of human constancy, everything *is* the same (29). This is a concept for which Stein was often ridiculed, and yet the simplicity of her statement is deceptive. All writers would have written quite differently had they lived in the era of another type of "composition." And yet, those qualities that are continuous in human experience make it possible for us to read the writers of the past with the feeling that they are relevant for us as readers in the present collective consciousness.

These speculations lead Stein directly to postulate the difference between a continuous and a prolonged present. Our conventional orientations tell us that time is composed of past, present, and future. Even though the present is the only moment we can know, it always recedes from the future and back into the past. It is impossible, therefore, to talk about a continuous present; for the one thing the present cannot do is continue. But, since the writer's job is to reflect his own time creatively, his works must exist completely in the present if they are to be authentic. The reader's experience of the work of art must also be in his own immediate present; it must not depend upon either memory or anticipation. Therefore, what the writer creates is a prolonged present, an extension of his *now*, since that is the only time in which he can authentically create. By corollary, any reader who experiences the presentness of a work also experiences the prolongation of this presentness throughout his own experiences as a reader. In order to create the prolonged present, the writer must continuously "begin again and again." In this way he continues what is always the same; yet by beginning again and again, he is constantly creating that which is new and continuously different.

The essay's final theory of importance concerns the way war speeds cultural change through developments in both technology and consciousness. War gives individuals in a culture something radically new to do, thereby changing the ways they see the world and creating a new "composition." In this way, too, Modernist artists were recognized more quickly and became "classics" more quickly than did most of the innovative artists of the past. Stein was quite moved by the fact that, without being a "successful" author in any commercial sense, she had been invited as a public figure and as a recognized innovator of twentieth-century consciousness to give an address at Cambridge. In this way, the war had speeded her own recognition. This theory also explains Hemingway's famous epigraph to *The Sun Also Rises:* Stein's statement, "You are all a lost generation." In referring to the young writers of her time, Stein claimed that they had been catapulted from youth to manhood without having had to go through the normal maturational process. The experience of the war had turned boys barely out of college into jaded adults by forcing them into a new consciousness.

II   Lectures in America

In the excitement following *The Autobiography of Alice B. Toklas,* Gertrude Stein made a lecture tour of the United States. Her talks were received with great enthusiasm everywhere and were published shortly thereafter as *Lectures in America.*[5] Printed in the form in which they were spoken, these lectures touch on almost every topic that interested Stein and are essential for a clear understanding of her thought.

The six titles — "What Is English Literature," "Pictures," "Plays," "The Gradual Making of The Making of Americans," "Portraits and Repetition," "Poetry and Grammar" — indicate that Stein's primary intention was to convey her central aesthetic concerns. Bridgman's description of the book as "a consideration of the modern movement in art as Gertrude Stein perceived and practiced it"[6] is both accurate and fair. Rediscovering the subject of herself while writing *The Autobiography of Alice B. Toklas,* Stein moved from that anecdotal consideration of her own personality and life to a theoretical examination of what most interested her. As with so many writers, Stein used her critical statements largely to justify her own practices, but she always illuminates along the way the general subject she is treating, even when her wise-child mannerisms lead to simplistic generalizations. Like most egocentric people, Stein was always more than willing to generalize from her own consciousness.

In the opening lecture, "What Is English Literature," Stein sought to answer this question by contrasting England and America geographically. Stein's leaps through English literary history are often breathtaking, especially since they are rarely accompanied by the usual evidence we expect in expository prose; for she mentions only a few authors. England has a "daily island life," she claims, and her culture has a kind of insular coherence that sprawling America lacks. In her theory, the richness of the developing English language afforded Chaucer a choice of colorful words that flowed into his poetry almost without effort. During the Renaissance, however, writers had to make more difficult choices among many words. By the Restoration, the basic syntactic unit of English had become the sentence because clarity and explanation were now the major literary goals. Stein relates this development to the growth of the British Empire which, according to Bridgman, "brought self-consciousness" (246) to the English people. But with continued imperial growth, explanation could no longer be satisfied by the shorter forms of syntax; therefore, by the end of the nineteenth century when Gertrude Stein came to her majority, the paragraph had become the major unit. Because the energies of the English had dissipated, the literature of the twentieth century was to be designed by an American; and Stein knew precisely which one — herself!

In this lecture, Stein develops her concept of the conflict between "god" and "mammon." The writer who serves "god" writes without regard for anything but the creative act itself, whereas the writer who serves "mammon" is conscious of an audience. Such a writer is a prisoner of convention and memory, a person corrupted by the impurity of his action. Like other militant turn-of-the-century innovators, Stein tried to be contemptuously independent of her audience. Because the new artists quite self-consciously wrote for a small coterie, they had to pretend to write for no one but themselves. Stein's reading of English literary history clearly had herself as its ultimate goal.

These principles of artistic integrity receive even stronger statement in "Pictures" in which Stein claims that the only reason for liking to look at paintings is that we like to do so. A painting must therefore give pleasure and hold the attention, but it is not required either to tell a story or to create an illusion of three-dimensionality; indeed, it is almost obliged to do neither. While Stein was willing to admit that resemblances between a painting and the real world often gave her pleasure, she was most concerned with the formal structures of the painting itself — the relationship of one part to another within the composition. Cézanne, she claimed, had taught her that all parts of a painting have equal value in terms of its composition. This lesson was, moreover, the most important one she had ever learned in relation to her own work; for as we have noted, her theory of painting definitely corresponds to her self-image of Gertrude Stein as a Modernist innovator.

The middle essays — "Plays" and "The Gradual Making of The Making of Americans" — are the least interesting. "Plays" too obviously rationalizes Stein's inability either to enjoy or to create conventional drama. She does explain what she does best in the theater, however, in creating the essences of static characters and landscapes. But, overall, Stein is clearly less at home with drama than with any other subject of her lectures. In a different way, "The Gradual Making of The Making of Americans" is also only partially successful. Because of the limited readers of her book, Stein obviously wanted to promote her longest work to her audiences; but her memories of the book, particularly of the order of its composition, were faulty; she was inclined, in addition, to quote too liberally from the text; and the book stimulated her into portentous generalizations about Americans that she had already expressed better in her opening lecture and that she was to improve on again in *The Geographical History of America*.

"Portraits and Repetition" was reputedly Stein's favorite lecture and has been judged by Richard Bridgman as the best of the lot. It is certainly as sustained and coherent a piece of prose as Stein ever wrote, perhaps because it presents material which she had already explored in "Composition as Explanation" and which she had ever since been thinking about. Returning to the theme of varied repetition in the midst of continuity, she now suggests that the rhythm of an individual's personality is determined by the continual way his behavior and consciousness are manifested but shift subtly from moment to moment, and from incident to incident. This suggestion is the perfect rationale for her having invented the portrait form to render the rhythm of personality because her gift for psychological insight is not limited in this form by the need either to make a plot or to involve herself in a long story in which memory or the other demands of "mammon" can charge their toll. Indeed, she saw her portraits as a perfect way for the writer to escape the tyranny of memory, for as a form they demand only a present act of creative consciousness. She saw *Tender Buttons* as her ultimate step in this direction.

The final lecture, "Poetry and Grammar," while perhaps the most

popular of these lectures, is primarily a *jeu d'esprit* in which Stein
elevates to a set of principles her grammatical and punctuational
idiosyncrasies. Stein claims that nouns form the basic vocabulary of
poetry, an assertion that would arouse an argument with a lot of
poets, but one that is understandable given Stein's concern with essences. Verbs are too active for anyone with Stein's concepts of
human psychology, a fact that becomes even clearer when we realize
that her favorite verb form is the participle, which is the verbal
closest to the noun. With regard to punctuation, however, Stein is
both more interesting and more conventional. She thinks of punctuation as primarily directions for when to take breath pauses, a
theory as commonplace as elementary school grammar. But she dis-
putes the need for some of the punctuational forms, particularly the
question mark and the comma. Periods she is willing to accept, but
question marks she objects to on aesthetic grounds. As for commas,
she seems to resent them deeply because, as she says, "A long complicated sentence should force itself upon you, make you know
yourself knowing it and the comma, well at the most a comma is a
poor period that it lets you stop and take a breath but if you want to
take a breath you ought to know yourself that you want to take a
breath"(221).

A look at Stein's Radcliffe themes will show the reader that she
always had trouble using commas with conventional propriety.[7] As
usual, it is difficult to take some of her assertions seriously since her
claims arise less from principle than from predisposition. Still, Stein
hits the mark with her claim that the fewer the commas the more the
reader must participate in the creative process, a claim consistent
with the desires of Picasso and others to force the viewer to organize
the fragmented Cubist painting in an act of participatory consciousness.

Lectures in America touches all the bases of Stein's aesthetic and
philosophical concerns, giving the author's own assessment of what
was central to her intellectual development. While Stein's
statements about herself must be taken, like anyone's self-appraisals,
with a handful of salt, they are a serious attempt by a major author to
explain herself. Like everything else of Stein's, these essays provide a
mixed pleasure; but they are the most accessible path into the
labyrinth of her ideas.

III   The Geographical History of America

Less accessible entries into Stein's thought are the pair of books
she wrote about the subject of identity during the middle 1930s, *The*

Geographical History of America and *Four in America.* While they are among her most difficult works, they also contain some of her most important ideas; and, because they contain variations about the same basic subject, they should be discussed in tandem. The former is a meditative philosophical discussion of the relationship of geography to personality and of the relationship of "human nature" to the "human mind." The latter is a fictionalized attempt to explore the relationships between names and social roles in four figures from American history. In the midst of much that is both banal and silly, Stein's wise-child pronouncements often convey genuinely profound thoughts about the basis of human personality and about the American character.

The full title of Stein's most elaborate treatise on human identity is *The Geographical History of America or the Relation of Human Nature to the Human Mind,*[8] but Stein says a great deal more about the latter half of her title than about the first. Published in 1936, this book discusses how the creative artist must discover his own abstract essence by isolating himself from the distressing messiness of ordinary life. For Stein, the human mind is the pure state of consciousness that an artist experiences in the act of creation. Human nature, whose characteristics are memory, emotion, and a concern with identity, is most like Stein's concept of "mammon"; it is clear that the human mind serves "god." It is only out of an act of pure contemplation that a work of art can truly emerge. Such a work may possibly be written *about* human nature, but never *by* human nature — only by human mind.

The two major and often repeated motifs of the book are expressed in "I am I because my little dog knows me" and "What is the use of being a little boy if you are going to grow up to be a man." The first expresses her idea of the essence of identity, which is the recognition by some consciousness outside the recognized individual. The need to be recognized in order to be sure of one's own existence Stein found troubling, but she obviously needed to understand this problem more and more after her extended recognition in the United States. She found that having to be continuously aware of an audience turned her into a creation by others rather than allowed her to create herself. It is one thing to learn from a dog's lapping water the difference between sentences and paragraphs, as Stein more than once claimed she had done; but it is quite another to let a dog's recognition be what determines the sense of self.

The other phrase reminds one of Yeats's concern in "Among School Children" of isolating being from the process of life: "How can you tell the dancer from the dance?" Stein's solution is different from the one Yeats implies; for her, life does consist of essences, or at least personality does; and the essence of a human being is determined when he is a child. But why should a person become what he is if what he is will change? This paradox of change within continuity is one that Stein has written about before, but the human mind is not concerned with such changes: it knows what it knows, and it is what it is. And what it knows, it knows by a supremely self-confident union with the object of its knowledge.

To understand a thing means to be in contact with that thing and the human mind can be in contact with anything.

Human nature can be connected with anything but it can not be in contact with anything. (38)

Because the human mind is not troubled by the problems of identity and emotions and can thus be fully conscious of its own being, it can have an empathetic experience of "contact" and thereby experience, create, and transmit genuine knowledge. But human nature, lacking this ability to detach itself from what makes anyone self-conscious — the messy experience of this world — cannot create genuine "connections" because it does not have the capacity for empathetic "contact."

It is clear that Stein felt herself to be a human mind, a pure experiencer of the world, serving "god" and creating works that have their own existence, like Kant's *ding an sich* ("thing in itself"). Why, she asks later in the book, "Why is it that in this epoch the only real literary thinking has been done by a woman" (182)? The answer Richard Bridgman gives connects Stein's conceptions of the human mind and American geography: "Although she did not directly say as much in this book, a portion of her answer would be that she had assumed creative leadership because she was an American. For Gertrude Stein championed the human mind because it reflected the American continent as she saw it during her visit to the United States. A great deal of flat land is connected with the human mind and so America is connected with the human mind" (264). Stein's epistemology, as usual, justifies her own method; and, as usual, she got tired by the end of the book; she concluded with the enigmatic statement: "I am not sure that is not the end" (207).

IV   Four in America

Four in America,[9] written a few years earlier, combines Stein's talents as a meditative theorist in psychology and cultural history, her skill as a portraitist, and her more limited ability in narrative fiction. As a result, it is impossible to classify the book. It could be discussed equally well in a number of contexts, but it is as a meditation on human identity that it is most successful. In *Four in America*, Stein is concerned with the ways that names and social roles establish an individual's sense of self. The idea for the book seems to have been generated by the fact that Ulysses S. Grant had originally been named Hiram Ulysses and that he had changed his name. Stein hypothesizes that, if Grant had not changed his name, he would have become a religious leader. This observation led her to contemplate what it would have been like if Grant had indeed been a religious leader, the Wright brothers painters, Henry James a general, and George Washington a novelist. The conception of the book is fascinating, but I agree with Bridgman that Stein was partially successful only with Grant and James and that she failed almost totally with the Wright brothers and Washington.

The style of *Four in America* is primarily that of nonlyrical meditative prose full of the most laborious repetitions, but what is most interesting about the book is that in the sections where Stein is most involved with her subject she manages to convey a sense of the inner reality of her historical subject and particularly of how the American character has shaped him. While what she says is often specious, particularly because she had not been to the United States in thirty years, she nonetheless manages to create both Grant and Henry James in genuine depth. The fact that she was a Civil War buff and a lifetime Jamesian means that she felt most at home with the material of these two sections. In *Four in America* Stein let her ideas about America and human identity run rampant. As a result, it is an exciting book but an ultimately unsatisfying one because it lacks any kind of genuinely formal development. Perhaps its most valuable contribution is the quirky but innovative way Stein has of dramatizing the ideas she expounds more fruitfully a few years later in *The Geographical History* and then in *Everybody's Autobiography*. The book also contains, like *The Geographical History*, an introduction by Thornton Wilder that is more helpful about Stein's work in general than about the specific content of *Four in America*.

V Narration

Narration[10] is a series of lectures Stein gave at the University of Chicago. These lectures for the most part treat material that Stein has covered elsewhere, particularly in *Lectures in America;* but they clarify many ideas and contain further thoughts about the nature of modern consciousness as well as some excellent insights into modern narrative. Like Marshall McLuhan two generations later, Stein maintains that the nineteenth-century ideal of a unified point of view and a chronologically continuous narrative is *passé*. To Stein, "Moving is in every direction" (19). Since the artist is the barometer of the culture, his writing must reflect its consciousness; therefore, narrative must no longer be obliged to provide a continuous line of development. She even suggests that a piece of writing need not have a beginning, middle, or end; it must exist simply on the basis of its internal balance from sentence to sentence. The work of art is autonomous and self-contained. These ideas are not new to Stein, but they are expressed more succinctly here than in *Lectures in America*.

Most of the final two untitled lectures are, as Bridgman has noted, somewhat incoherent. Either Stein ran out of things to say or she lowered her controls a bit, and permitted all her current ideas to race out onto the page. At any rate, most of what the reader finds valuable in *Narration* appears in the first half, along with the usual Thornton Wilder introduction. In fairness to Stein, however, she was exploiting the same vein as in *Lectures in America, Four in America,* and *The Geographical History of America*. Since her theory was that the artist's creation deals with the present contents of his consciousness, she was trapped by this rationalization into publishing anything she wrote. And since she was at the peak of her new popularity, she allowed herself to be exploited into writing more than she should have. We should be thankful, however, for the industry with which she produced these explanations; for they constitute, with all their excesses, one of the most spirited defenses of the Modernist attitude as well as the best introduction to the thought of Modernism's most demanding figure, Gertrude Stein.

VI   The Autobiography of Alice B. Toklas

The works on which most readers' contact with Stein is based and on which her reputation will no doubt continue to flourish are her memoirs of the world of modern art; of Paris, the center of that world; of Picasso, the leading figure of that world; and of France during World War I. These books are *The Autobiography of Alice B. Toklas, Everybody's Autobiography, Picasso* (the only book Stein wrote in French), *Paris France,* and *Wars I Have Seen,* all of which have been recently reprinted. Of all Stein's works these are not only the most easily understandable, but they also present most directly the aura surrounding the myth of the high priestess of Modernism.

It is difficult to imagine a more unlikely best-selling author than Gertrude Stein, and yet in 1933 *The Autobiography of Alice B. Toklas* was a literary sensation. Even today it remains the most widely read of all Stein's books. On the surface, *The Autobiography* is a witty, somewhat malicious collection of gossip and anecdotes about a number of the figures of Modernist art, all of whom manage somehow to orbit around Gertrude Stein. Its initial popularity was surely due to the fact that the public was hungry for scandalous information about Bohemian life in Paris. Prepared for the book by excerpts published in *The Atlantic*, the American reading public put *The Autobiography* on the best-seller list and kept it there for a while.

But four decades later it is clear that the lasting esteem in which the book is held is due to more than its being *succès de scandale*. Alice Toklas's "autobiography" is a complex, carefully constructed book that shows remarkable narrative sophistication; but it leaves something to be desired as history, particularly in its cavalier treatment of matters of fact. A year after its great success, Eugene and Mary Jolas — editors of *transition,* the most famous of the exile literary journals — published a supplement entitled *Testimony against Gertrude Stein*[11] in which figures like Matisse, Georges Braque, and Tristan Tzara counter-attacked by pointing out somewhat feebly *The Autobiography's* factual errors. But, while this kind of carping is quite understandable, it misses the point of what Stein was doing and proves the validity of her method.

Stein's form was the memoir, not a history; but her technique was fictional from the start, and its aim was both personal publicity and self-justification. In addition, Braque's accusation that she understood the Modernist movement purely in terms of personalities is quite the point. Although she made elaborate pretensions to objectivity, Stein saw everything through subjective eyes; and she was much less adept at sustained detachment than she was at seeing the relationship of ideas and personality. Her serene and almost absurd egoism always placed her at the center of events in Paris during the century's early years; as a result, she omitted any mention by name of Leo, Michael, or Sarah Stein in order to give the impression that Gertrude Stein alone had discovered modern painting.

The major narrative device of *The Autobiography of Alice B. Toklas* is also its chief literary trick — that of pretending the narrative voice belongs not to Gertrude Stein but to Alice Toklas. To those who knew Alice, Stein's imitation of her manner of speaking is almost perfect; and those readers of Alice's later memoir, *What Is Remembered,*[12] notice similarities in the conciseness of phrasing and in the astringency of wit. Some recent critics have raised the serious question of whether Alice did not indeed write some or perhaps all of the "autobiography" herself; and the most elaborate discussion of this problem is by Richard Bridgman (209 - 17), who has examined the manuscripts. Although Bridgman raises the question, he draws no definitive conclusions; and I see no reason from his evidence to doubt that Stein did write the book herself, although as always she relied on Alice's sense of fact and of detail as well as of taste. Stein's ear was always remarkable, and her use in this case of another person's speech patterns enabled her to write a sustained piece of narrative that is, for once, consistent in style and that rarely flags in either energy or reader interest.

By using the voice of someone only on the fringes of Modernism, Stein was able to minimize the sound of her own partisanship and self-puffery. Several passages would be quite ludicrous if written directly by the author, but somehow the voice of Alice makes it possible for us to read them without cringing. One of the book's most notorious assertions is a case in point: "I may say that only three times in my life have I met a genius and each time a bell within me rang and I was not mistaken, and I may say in each case it was before there was any general recognition of the quality of genius in them. The three geniuses of whom I wish to speak are Gertrude Stein, Pablo Picasso and Alfred Whitehead" (5). By transferring her monumental egotism to another voice, Stein much more easily places herself at the center of every crucial situation in the book and makes her own eminence seem simply natural.

The two most fascinating parts of the narrative are the early section about life in Paris during the first fifteen years of this century and the later section which relates the coming of the expatriates to the same city just after World War I. The main hero of the early part, other than Stein herself, is Pablo Picasso; and Stein's strategy is to insist that her development and Picasso's were parallel in inventing the new century's consciousness. As usual, Stein writes without serious regard for the actual facts; she prefers to repeat discredited stories as long as they add to the myth she is trying to create. For instance, she repeats the story of Guillaume Apollinaire's coming home to cheering crowds at the Armistice just before his death when she must have known quite well that her friend had died two days before.

But, as George Wickes points out,[13] the myth of the Modernist movement was more important to her than the actual facts; and myth, after all, is the most profound variety of truth. Stein was not testifying before a jury; she was telling a story and creating a consciousness. Her version, for instance, of the "banquet" in honor of the "douanier" Henri Rousseau is the most amusing and readable account of that event we have. Although the story was also retold by Fernande Olivier,[14] Picasso's former mistress, in the same year as Alice's "autobiography" and repeated many other times since (including the account in Roger Shattuck's *The Banquet Years*),[15] no other single account of that event has had as much impact as Stein's has had, inaccurate in detail as it may be. The banquet did occur, and some of the events during it are not in question. What *exactly* did happen we shall never know. But, as an event whose absurd gaiety symbolizes the meaning of those early days of Modernism, the banquet, in Stein's rendering, is crucial to our understanding the spirit of Picasso, Stein, Max Jacob, and the rest of that marvelous group.

What I am suggesting is that we should do our best to read this "autobiography" with some of the critical tools we bring to a work of fiction. By creating a narrative persona, Stein was quite knowingly using a fictional technique; and by continuously turning the events she lived through into occasions for narrative presentation, Stein was also exercising a prerogative of the *roman à clef*. Our demands for accuracy and fairness must take second place to our demands for the writing to be interesting, the structure coherent, the observations memorable. On all the latter counts, *The Autobiography of Alice B. Toklas* is a resounding success.

The book's seven chapters are not always arranged chronologically; their shiftings in time are dependent upon how Stein had to strike a balance between the chapters in which she appeared without Alice and those in which Miss Toklas was finally on the scene. Some of the most memorable events, particularly the purchases of the first paintings of Cézanne, Matisse, and Picasso, occurred before Alice came to Paris sometime around 1907. The reader is brought up to date on these matters and on such other occasions as Stein's posing for Picasso when it seems dramatically feasible and not as chronology demands. The simple listing of the chapter titles gives the reader a sense of how Stein went about organizing her narrative: "Before I

Came to Paris," "My Arrival in Paris," "Gertrude Stein in Paris
1903 - 1907," "Gertude Stein before She Came to Paris," "1907 -
1914," "The War," "After the War 1919 - 1932."
   The actual style is surprisingly straightforward and free of most of
Stein's usual idiosyncrasies. Although there are punctuational eccen-
tricities, Stein uses standard English in her wise-child tone; but she
nonetheless rigidly maintains Alice Toklas's point of view. There is
almost no mystification or deliberate ambiguity, although some of
the insights are occasionally oblique. Stein writes with continuous
good humor and high spirits, even though she is often malicious in
settling scores with those people she does not like. Shifting alliances
and changing friendships had always been concerns of Stein's, as the
evidence of *Q. E. D.* makes clear; and the sting of her wit in the
"autobiography" was felt by Ezra Pound and Glenway Wescott, by
Matisse and his wife, by Fernande Olivier and André Salmon, and
most of all, later in the book, by Ernest Hemingway. Constantly ad-
vising Hemingway that "Remarks are not literature," Stein nonetheless makes a literature of her own witty remarks, such as
"Glenway Wescott has a certain syrup but it doesn't pour."
   But it is against Hemingway that she mounts her heaviest verbal
arsenal. There is something wistful about the changes Stein portrays
in Paris following World War I. Something is gone from the lively,
heady sense of fun that characterized her early days there. The war is
at fault; so is the fact of the great commercial successes of Picasso
and Matisse; and so for that matter is the notoriety that Stein had
achieved even before her own great success with this very book. The
young men after the war were serious, a generation deprived of its
youth, and the most serious of these serious young men was the
Hemingway whom Stein claims to have taught everything he knew.
   When their relationship turned sour, Stein turned heavily against
the more famous and financially successful younger writer. There
are sour grapes here, although Hemingway himself was in the habit
of biting the hands that had helped him — his falling out with
Sherwood Anderson and the vicious but funny (and deserved)
parody of Anderson in *The Torrents of Spring*. Stein thought she was
getting in the last word, and she periodically made remarks about
her protege in the years following *The Autobiography*. The partisans
on either side mount impressive arguments for their heroes,
although both writers had a streak of petulance that makes it difficult to sympathize with either one — not that it makes any difference. The egos of writers are notoriously complex and vulnerable.

Hemingway himself continued the battle in *The Green Hills of Africa* and *Death in the Afternoon,* for his feelings were perhaps doubly sensitized because he so clearly owed something to Stein's tutelage.[16] And because he lived longer than Stein, he managed to have the last word in *A Moveable Feast*[17] in a brilliant, thoroughly malicious memoir about Stein and Alice that is probably as historically valid as the remembrances in *The Autobiography* but that is nonetheless equally memorable and just as well written a piece of fiction.

The controversy still continues, however, as a recent essay by Donald Sutherland attests.[18] Sutherland, who was a close acquaintance of Stein's, as well as one of her important critics, continued as confidant to Alice Toklas after Gertrude's death. He wrote in 1971 of a conversation he had with Alice in 1966 just before she died; she confided that it was she who had managed the dismissal of Hemingway from Stein's life. The reason was that Hemingway and Stein were highly attracted to each other and on the verge of an affair. Toklas even thought that Stein and Hemingway might marry (he was married at the time to Hadley Richardson, his first wife). Sutherland is scrupulous about suggesting that the affair was probably not consummated and is also a bit skeptical about Toklas's interpretation of the whole business. If it is true that Stein and Hemingway were more than just casually attracted (at the time Stein was about fifty and Hemingway half that age), their being so would explain the catty way they later spoke about each other. It would also explain Hemingway's petulant dismissal of Toklas in his memoirs; for he reports that she once put Stein down profanely when Hemingway and Hadley were at their apartment.

That Alice had some justification in feeling her own "marriage" threatened is borne out in the recent biography by James Mellow, *Charmed Circle: Gertrude Stein & Company,* the best life yet of Stein. He reports that Hemingway wrote in a letter to W. G. Rogers, the book reviewer, of a final meeting he and Stein had during World War II, in which they "had agreed that they still loved one another. In his letter, Hemingway paid Gertrude the ultimate masculine compliment, saying that he had always had an urge to fuck her. Gertrude, he maintained, was well aware of this; it established a healthy bond between them. He attributed their former break to," among other things, "Alice's jealousy of any of Gertrude's real men-friends. . . . "[19] Perhaps Hemingway was merely beating his chest in this letter, but Alice's capacity for malice took a back seat to no one's, and Hemingway was definitely not one of her favorite people. Even in letters written long after Gertrude's death Alice continued to express acidic judgments against him. One wonders as well about what attracted he-man Hemingway to such a figure of ambivalent sexuality, who even in the twenties was quite openly known as involved in a homosexual marriage. But then I am far from the first person to wonder about the nature of Hemingway's repressions.

It is doubtful that any of the principals can be relied on for the facts; and, although it is always fascinating to speculate about the private lives of such celebrities as Stein and Hemingway, the truth about their relationship and their statements will probably remain unknown. What does remain are the fascinating memoirs left by each of the famous authors, and we must not lose sight of the genuine reasons why we enjoy them.

While it is fashionable among some Stein *aficionados* to denigrate *The Autobiography* as mere "entertainment," we should not be such snobs as to insist that Stein be approached only through works written in her abstract style. *The Autobiography of Alice B. Toklas* is a masterful performance; it is quite the most important memoir of any Modernist figure; and it is unique in its literary innovation. Stein has created in it not only a most viable myth of Paris as the seat of Modern Art, but also an unforgettable myth of "Gertrude Stein," a myth that has threatened the serious understanding of her work and may always be larger than the intrinsic significance of any of her "creative" performances. This problem she herself understood, and it concerned her throughout the rest of her career.

VII   Everybody's Autobiography

Everybody's Autobiography[20] is a sequel to *The Autobiography of Alice B. Toklas;* and while (like most sequels) it is not as good as the original, the book is still much more than a failure. In writing her first "autobiography," Stein discovered a talent her friends had long known about from her conversation: Stein was a marvelous raconteur who combined wit and narrative skill. Although *Everybody's Autobiography* is more loosely constructed than Alice Toklas's, it is quite humorous in its own way, and its reminiscences are almost as memorable even though Stein had already used much of her best material.

She seems to have viewed the problem confronting her in the new book as an obligation to find another autobiographical style. The transition from the first autobiography to the style she used in

Everybody's Autobiography is fairly obvious, although the change was certainly not easy. In the first book, she had quite successfully mimicked the voice of her lifelong companion; in the new autobiography, she decided to mimic the voice of herself in conversation. Both the quoted reports of Stein in conversation by such people as Thornton Wilder and the style of *Everybody's Autobiography* are quite similar. The reader has the overwhelming sense in reading the latter book that he is eavesdropping on a Stein monologue. To mimic her own conversational tone in writing was not so easy as the reader might imagine; but Stein was certainly able to manage it.

A comparision of the sentence structures in each book makes clear just what the reader's problems are in regard to the change in style. The sentences here are long and punctuated with great eccentricity, much more so than in the first autobiography. These statements are also full of parenthetical statements, asides, tangents, and even *non sequiturs*. To come upon this voice after Alice Toklas's is to be puzzled at first; the very form of the sentences is exhausting, as is the consciousness that seems at first unable to stick to the subject. But this impression is only a preliminary illusion. The book is really quite tightly organized, even if its narrator's associational patterns seem arbitrary, and the narrative progresses steadily. Stein circles her subject, moving out from it to connected associations, but she always returns to the original material.

The book is concerned with the events of the two years following the publication of *The Autobiography of Alice B. Toklas*, including the production of *Four Saints in Three Acts* and the American lecture tour. Stein is concerned primarily with the effect of her sudden notoriety on her sense of identity; and, as we have seen many times, Stein's focus throughout the 1930s was on this problem. In *Everybody's Autobiography*, Stein gets down to specifics; and by generalizing her own identity crises, Stein justifies the book's title. Everybody is concerned with who he is and with how the circumstances of his life affect his sense of identity; therefore, an autobiography concerned with such a problem is really everybody's autobiography and not just Gertrude Stein's. Stein's willingness to use herself as a source from which to generalize places her in a great American tradition with such writers as Walt Whitman and Thomas Wolfe, Henry Thoreau, and Henry Miller.

The organizing principle of *Everybody's Autobiography* is chronological. With seemingly exhaustive detail, Stein goes through a description of the day-to-day activities with which she and Alice

filled their days in Bilignin. There is very little about their life in
Paris here. But interspersed throughout the book, as tangents and
associations either to events or themes, are memories of her childhood; and these are much more specific and personal in tone than
anything that had appeared in her previous memoirs. She mentions
all her brothers and her one sister, and she expresses quiet remorse
that she would never see Leo again. She is quite honest about their
closeness both as children and as adults during their first years
together in Paris. Whether this impression is just the difference
between Alice's snappish sensibility and the more relaxed and
phlegmatic temperament of Gertrude Stein it is hard to be sure, but
the tone of this book is quite serene. Such serenity makes us uneasy,
for we find it difficult to accept the calmness that Stein projects: she
wants too much to be an unruffled middle-aged self. But she takes
her time, she does not get excited, and the roundabout garrulity of
her voice injects a steadily humorous bemusement rather than a
sharp, witty commentary about the proceedings. Because of a surprising lack of epigrams in this book, we are concerned with human
comedy, not the wit of a twentieth-century La Rochefoucauld. Although *Everybody's Autobiography* is much less brilliant than the
first autobiography, it is a much solider book.

Although this work is carefully wrought, the selection of details
seems almost intentionally random. Amid the supposedly more
serious matters of writing, publishing, having a play produced, and
planning a lecture tour, we are told even more about shopping, cooking, clothing, servants, and auto repairs. Why not? The quotidian
makeup of all human lives, even those of celebrities, is embodied in
precisely this kind of detail. The great event is rare for everyone. For
Stein, all human events are equal and should be treated equally,
much like all the parts of a Cézanne painting. Even in the book's
most interesting section, which tells in detail about Stein's
triumphant lecture tour, the author spends as much time talking
about what people wear, what their homes look like, and what kind
of food she got at every stop along the way. She repeats conversations she had with ordinary people on the street, with both garage
mechanics and celebrities; and she treats everyone with equal
reverence. Stein is an American democrat.

In addition, this is definitely a book of the 1930s. The world outside Stein's consciousness obtrudes into her narrative constantly
through her many observations about social conditions, about the
Spanish revolution that was to become a civil war, about money

(about which she was a fiscal conservative). She constantly gives the impression of someone who not only observes the world but positively absorbs it.

Still, for all its good humor and lightness of tone, this is basically a serious book — occasionally an almost solemn one. Stein is, in this book as elsewhere, a meditator; and she reveals herself as someone who was even as a child of a meditative bent. She concerns herself not only with identity, but with why — because of electric lights — dogs no longer bay at the moon; with the problems of death and an afterlife; with murders, fame, and sainthood. At the approach of her own old age, she is much more inclined to meditate about the mortality of others and particularly about violence. While Stein was publicly incapable of humility until the end of her life, she was capable in this book — for the first time it seems to me — of a genuinely statesmanlike attitude toward others, toward her own life, and toward living in general. I agree with the surprise of Richard Bridgman when he wonders why this book has not been taken more seriously until now (see 269 - 284). It is, once the reader masters the conversational tone, one of Stein's most interesting, perhaps even most important, works. Ironically, for a writer who began her career in an intense effort to excise as much of the external world as possible from her works, Stein emerges late in life as one of the finest chroniclers of the world in which she happened to be living.

VIII   Picasso

Stein's next narrative of meditative criticism and reminiscence was the short book *Picasso*, which was written and published initially (in 1938) in French.[21] Stein had some problems with her French since she wrote in it so seldom, but Alice corrected some of her more egregious grammatical errors. This personal book is full of anecdotes and is written in a familiar tone. A committed student of a friend's work, Stein does not say much that is new about Picasso's art; but she does manage to convey an intense understanding of what he was trying to do. Of all the short books written about Picasso, this one is as good as any to read as an introduction. The illustrative paintings are well chosen, and the text is one of the clearest Stein was ever to write.

One reason for the seeming simplicity of Stein's prose is the fact that, writing in French, she used much less complex diction and syntax. Another reason, and one just as important, is that Stein had been writing and lecturing constantly about many of the book's ideas during the previous decade. Familiar to readers of her other works are her theories about the infrequency of masterpieces, the nature of the truly creative mind that chooses "god" over "mammon," and the nature of identity. We hear once more about why America and Spain were the places most conditioned by their cultures to give birth to the founders of twentieth-century art, and her nominees are herself and her subject, Picasso.

I do not wish to demean what Stein is doing. As a matter of fact, her abstract theories work very well in dealing with Picasso's work. For instance, her theory of the "human mind" enables her to have the following insight about how Picasso's imagination works visually rather than literarily: ". . . Picasso when he saw an eye, the other one did not exist for him and only the one he saw did exist for him and as a painter, and particularly as a Spanish painter, he was right, one sees what one sees, the rest is a reconstruction from memory and painters have nothing to do with memory, they concern themselves only with visible things . . ." (15). The "human mind," the consciousness of the saint and of the creative artist, perceives the world directly; it does not need recourse to what is remembered — thus the visual freshness of the new painting, what Stein was ironically to call its "ugliness."

She again combines her theory of the "human mind" with an almost specious generalization about Spanish culture to suggest quite provocatively how Modernist art has rejected the past: "Related things are things remembered and for a creator, certainly for a Spanish creator, certainly for a Spanish creator of the twentieth century, remembered things are not things seen, therefore they are not things known" (35). Stein's theories and her instincts work well together. We do not have the feeling, as in so many books about painters, that a brilliant intellectual insight about the nature of "art" has little to do with the actual pieces executed by the artist.

Stein is also sensitive about the problems of identity that Picasso suffered. She tells of how Picasso stopped painting for a time during the 1930s and began to write poetry. But the poetry was a painter's poetry and not a poet's, for painters and writers, Stein claims, perceive the world with different sensory orientations. She could understand a hiatus during an artist's career, since she herself had trouble writing for a while after the *Autobiography*, but to turn to another art for which a person's sensibility makes one unsuited is a mistake. People are what they are, which is determined by the nature of their consciousness; and Picasso was a painter who needed a rest from painting to see the world freshly. He did not need to start working in a medium in which he was condemned to be mediocre. Stein implies that it was her advice that got Picasso back to painting again.

Finally, an artist is most important to the world as a barometer of what is going on in the culture — the "composition" — of his generation. "A creator," she says, "is not in advance of his generation but he is the first of his contemporaries to be conscious of what is happening to his generation" (30). This role she tried very hard to fulfill herself, and in this book — ironically, a work of retrospection — she manages to convey quite skillfully the role that her good friend played in shaping the collective imagination of their century.

IX Paris France

Stein's lifelong love affair with her adopted country is best expressed in another short book, *Paris France*,[22] published two years after *Picasso*. This sunny account — written in simple, clear diction — is, as Richard Bridgman rightly observes, not about Paris so much as it is about "the French character" (296). The optimism and sanguine smugness with which Stein writes about her France belies the fact that the book was written after the beginning of World War II. Since Stein still clung to the France in which she had lived for almost forty years, her book has such a curious detachment from world affairs that it seems like wishful thinking.

As usual, Stein is most concerned with her theory of culture and how she, Gertrude Stein, managed to be in exactly the right place in order to invent the modern consciousness. *The Geographical History of America* had claimed the United States for the human mind; *Paris France* claims France for human nature. But France is a place where human nature has been accommodated so well that life has been raised to a fine art; and, as a result, the human mind can function better there than anywhere else. America is a land of publicity and no privacy, but "publicity in France is really not important, tradition and their private life and the soil which always produces something, that is what counts" (10).

Throughout the book Stein plays the role of bourgeois conservative, for she claims that only within an elaborate social structure and traditional rules can man be free. In her eyes France, by providing such a situation, gave Stein the freedom to create: "I cannot write too much upon how necessary it is to be completely conservative that is particularly traditional in order to be free. And so

France is and was. Sometimes it is important and sometimes it is not, but from 1900 to 1939, it certainly was" (38). The French attitude toward science and technology is also important in this regard: "The reason why all of us naturally began to live in France is because France has scientific methods, machines and electricity, but does not really believe that these things have anything to do with the real business of living. Life is tradition and human nature" (8). A country like the United States that lacks a fixed culture is much more likely to be transformed by its response to technological change. But an established country like France can assimilate change more easily; and, for an artist, a fixed point is necessary in order for change to be both measurable and meaningful. Stein relates these changes in twentieth-century consciousness to developments in Modernist painting: "The twentieth century was not interested in impressions, it was not interested in emotions it was interested in conceptions and so there was the twentieth century painting (61). Twentieth-century painting is a creation of the human mind, but that of the nineteenth was created by human nature.

As for the importance of the interest in "conceptions" to twentieth-century artists, "These conceptions all have to do with the world being round and everybody knowing all about it and there being illimitable space and everybody knowing all about it and if anybody knows all about the world being round and all about illimitable space the first thing they do is to paint their conceptions of these things and that the twentieth century painting did (61-62). The artist as barometer of his race must record the twentieth-century *angst* about infinity. But, according to Stein, the French, who have remained tightly tied to the soil, have not as a people been disoriented by these developments. As a result, they can provide the ideal middle-class stability in which an artist can contemplate the disorientations to which the world subjects him.

This France not all observers would recognize, for Stein is projecting many of her own bourgeois needs on to her adopted land. Stein carried her own space with her, and she needed the France she described even if it did not altogether exist. The most convincing parts of her book have less to do with her cultural theories than with the sense she gives of the characteristics of French everyday life — one to which she was equipped by temperament to respond. Her felt senses of the French family and of the delights of French cuisine are genuine, much more so than the myth of France she creates to justify her sojourn there. A far better sense of what the creative life of Paris was in the early years of this century is contained in *The Autobiography of Alice B. Toklas*. *Paris France* remains a charming book, but it adds little to our knowledge of France or to our insights into Stein's thought.

X Wars I Have Seen

Wars I Have Seen[23] is a much more ambitious work. When published, it was highly successful; it achieved bestseller status for a while; by and large, it received impressive reviews; but it is a book that does not wear very well for the contemporary reader. Beginning it sometime in 1943 as a kind of daybook or journal, Stein continued it for fifteen months; and she decided not to stop it until the German occupation was at an end. The narrative's subject matter is once again the quotidian details of everyday life in rural France during the occupation.

For the student of Stein, this book is an interesting chronicle of the contents of her consciousness during her last years. Removed from their home in Bilignin because the landlord needed the house, Stein and Alice moved to Culoz, an even smaller village where they stayed for the remainder of the war. In one sense they showed great courage, for the position of two old Jewish women during the German occupation was not exactly a relaxed one. But they both resisted entreaties to flee to Switzerland, perhaps as much out of inertia as principle; for they preferred to remain in a world they knew and among people to whom they were used rather than to risk the uncertainties of a more distant exile. In an occupied country, however, the matters of Modernist literature and authorial reputation seem somehow irrelevant. In such an existence even the so-called principles on which the war is supposed to be fought do not always have meaning. What does matter is what has always mattered; where the next food is coming from, the neighborhood and village intrigues, and the necessities — shoes, clothing, cooking. Certainly Stein's is one of the few books to come out of World War II with such an emphasis.

The narrative, although its continuity is fractured as a journal would normally be, is written in one continuous chapter without a single break. The only pauses come with the paragraphing, a fact that makes the book a long draught for one sitting, especially with Stein's growing penchant for long sentences with few commas, a mannerism extended from *Everybody's Autobiography*. Stein does not record a date for each day; instead, she only announces the first of each new month. For the most part, the prose is free of "Stein-ese," although there are occasions when she seems to tire of making a lengthy point and lapses into one of her poetic styles: "And at the end of babyhood to fourteen, at the end there is nothing in between. What did she say when she was fourteen. She said she was not will-ing to be a queen. And he, he was not interested in a king or a queen not when he was fourteen. Not at all. And in this way from fifteen to twenty-four began and it began with also ran" (26). Rhymes and puns are never completely gone from Stein's work; but, by and large, the style of *Wars I Have Seen* is closer to the prose of *Everybody's Autobiography* than to anything else; but it is also more solemn.

The generalizing Stein does adds little to her established theories. She still thinks that centuries are separate cultural entities, and she spends a large amount of space in this book telling about how World War II brought about the end of the nineteenth century. Once again, Stein feels herself ideally placed to describe the emergence of modern culture. In addition, she repeats in *Wars I Have Seen* a number of anecdotes familiar to readers of both *Paris France* and *Everybody's Autobiography*, particularly one about a French far-mer's comments relative to German propensity for dictatorship:

There was a farmer who once said to me he said it in 1941, he said they say it is Hitler, but it is not Hitler. I fought all the other war and I know what Ger-mans are. They are a funny people. They are always choosing some one to lead them in a direction which they do not want to go. They cannot help themselves they are not led, it is not the Kaiser, it is not Hitler, who leads them, it is they themselves who choose the man and really force him to lead them in a direction which they do not want to go. (64)

This anecdote appears more than once in the book, and its apologetic tone for the German people is symptomatic of the general tone of acceptance that Stein adopts throughout *Wars I Have Seen*. There is little that is meaningful in wars, in the reasons they are fought, or in life itself for that matter. This resignation is not just cynical; it is the tone of old age that counter-balances the wise-child pose of the narrator. For a long time, Stein refuses partisanship one way or another; she knows that the realities of life in war and peace are basically the same, that the moral differences between people in one country and in another are insignificant, and that it is too easy to blame the enemy for all the world's evils. As a result, Stein presents a number of lame defenses of German anti-Semitism; and she never directly acknowledges that she herself is Jewish.

Stein is least good at generalizing in *Wars I Have Seen,* but she is quite good at describing not only the small details in her own life, but also in telling the stories of life in the village, particularly about the intrigues surrounding the Resistance fighters, the *maquis.* Only gradually does she begin to take sides against the Germans and to support the simple country patriots of Culoz. Stein's greatest annoyance often seems directed against the restraints imposed by wartime, particularly by the notorious French bureaucrats. She finds it somewhat difficult when everything is rationed to be concerned with French independence, but the childishness of Stein's self-indulgence is probably not atypical of what people must be like in such conditions. The brute facts of the war existed on the battlefield, and there were only occupation forces in the village. The men of the village were often forced into munition plants or into the Vichy army, but these facts seem like minor annoyances in Stein's narrative. Stein becomes increasingly annoyed with the Germans as the war drags on and as it becomes clear that they will lose.

It is difficult to sympathize with such expedient shifts in attitude. Bridgman sees Stein's adaptability as "dangerously close to sycophancy" (330), and it is true that her enthusiasm for the coming of the Americans increases steadily as they are obviously winning the war. The irony is that Stein emerged at the end of the war as a mother figure for "G. I. Joe" and was as unabashedly patriotic as any salesman of Liberty Bonds in the epilogue to *Brewsie and Willie.* But the key to this change in attitude lies in a larger need that she had — her need for publicity and recognition. I agree with Bridgman's feeling that, with the coming of the Americans, Stein could emerge from the obscurity of her provincial exile into a world where she was once again a "lion." The soldiers had heard of her, and she was interviewed and invited to speak on Armed Forces Radio. Stein's final perorations in this book on the subject of freedom have to be seen in this context.

What is finally interesting in *Wars I Have Seen* is the unprotected way in which the author exposes herself. Because it is a journal, Stein does not adopt a literary persona to protect her from her own inconsistencies and pettinesses. As an honest record of the shifting feelings of someone of literary sensibility marooned in a French village for three years as she approached and passed the age of seventy, *Wars I*

Have Seen is an unusual and sometimes impressive literary document. There is no account of World War II quite like it. It is most profound when it tries least to be, and its human warmth and basic tolerance show Stein to be a simpler person than she often pretended. Its mixture of bitterness and resignation — with a stronger emphasis on the latter — goes hand in hand with what we have seen in *The Mother of Us All*. The Mother of Modernism was trying once again to sum up and explain her own struggle for identity and, by corollary, the struggle of all modern individuals for the same thing, individuals for whom she had always felt herself the representative.

CHAPTER 8

Conclusion

ON 3 February 1974, Gertrude Stein, if she had lived, would
have been one hundred years old. It is pleasant to believe that,
just like her friend Pablo Picasso, she would have gone on creating
new styles even when past the age of ninety. But, although we may
lament Stein's ultimate mortality, she did manage to live a long and
highly productive life. Any assessment of artists like Stein and
Picasso is made more complicated than usual by the strange fact that
the innovations of early Modernist art retain a kind of startling
freshness that seems quite rare, even unique, in the history of art.
Readers in 1903, for instance, saw the work of Ralph Waldo Emerson
as quite definitely that of a long previous age, just as today we tend
to see the tales of Stephen Crane and the novels of Theodore
Dreiser, two other recent centenarians. But we can still hear heated
arguments about the validity of the innovations of Stein and Picasso,
Matisse and Joyce; and these are artists, we must remember, much
of whose major work is now more than half a century old.

Innovative Modernism is clearly still disturbing for people who
are as yet unwilling to accept the attitude that perspective and the
single point of view are only dated conventions. Even to those of us
for whom acceptance is not an issue, early Modernist art remains
amazingly disorienting; for we cannot yet relax in complete comfort
within the world of fragmentation. And yet, it is also clear that
Modernism does have something we can call a "classical" style to
which we have by now become somewhat accustomed and against
which we measure works created more recently in both conventional
and experimental modes. It is among the "classic" writers of
Modernism that Gertrude Stein belongs; perhaps because — to
apply her own criteria — her work has by this time ceased to appear
as "ugly" as it used to.

The intention of this critical-analytical study of Stein has been to reestablish the nature of her "ugliness" as well as the historical reasons for both its emergence and its disorienting effect on her contemporaries. But, before concluding, we should explore one more question: What is the source of Stein's appeal to, and importance for, readers today? For it is clear that, in spite of all the controversy that still surrounds her name, Stein's work is now being read and discussed more than ever before.

There is probably no other writer who would be less comprehensible without reference to the time (the "composition") in which she wrote. While it may be a tautology to say that writers reflect their time and milieu, there are still certain periods of the past in which cultural upheaval seems, in retrospect, so apparent and inescapable that the works of art created during that time become functions of that revolution. During such epochs, certain writers emerge who can be best appreciated only within the context of that release of cultural energy, just as there are others who, in following these pioneers, become writers for all ages. For example, Christopher Marlowe is for the English Renaissance a writer of the first category; and Shakespeare quite clearly belongs to the second. This is not to say that Marlowe is not an important author; he certainly is — and, had he lived longer, his accomplishments would surely have been even more substantial. But had Marlowe not lived at all, Shakespeare's own work would probably not have assumed the shape it did; for Shakespeare was able to surpass his predecessor only by absorbing his innovations. Marlowe is clearly a catalytic figure for both Shakespeare and the English Renaissance, particularly in the drama; and this function is at least as important as the creation of *Doctor Faustus* or *Edward II*.

It does not seem outlandish to suggest that Stein occupies a similar position in Modernist literature. Like "an event in chemistry,"[1] she seems in retrospect to have been an inevitable product of cultural energy. Heir to a century of Romanticism and its implications for authorial subjectivity and experimentation, and versed also in modern psychology, Stein had the good fortune to be drawn to an environment, Paris, where innovators in the other arts were attempting experiments similar to hers that ultimately changed the way all civilized peoples were to see and create the world. Her relationship with Picasso was crucial in this regard; for, beginning with "Melanctha," Stein's writings quite often went through the same stages of experimentation as the paintings of her Spanish friend.

Because of her connections with Modernist painting, Stein was the first writer in English that I know of who came to see writing as *purely* a problem in composition; and her explorations of the limits of the English language made it possible for a number of important writers to go to school to her. Sherwood Anderson, as early as 1920, wrote of how crucial for his own style had been the influence of *Three Lives* and *Tender Buttons*.[2] It is impossible to conceive of the mature work of Ernest Hemingway without taking into consideration the direct effect of Stein's tutelage on him, the young expatriate. That *The Sun Also Rises* now seems to most readers more accomplished and interesting than anything Stein wrote is one of those ironic curve balls history seems fond of throwing at the innovative.

The fact that the work of younger writers who composed in the spirit of Modernism, men like Hemingway and Anderson, was more immediately attractive and accessible to most readers spread the acceptance of Modernism and also enabled the greater part of a few generations to dismiss Stein as an eccentric of limited literary importance. But, paradoxically, it is also true that, by accepting many of Stein's experiments as part of their literary conventions, these writers have made it possible for us to understand for the first time much of what Stein was doing. Imitation is more than simply flattery; it is the most important kind of acceptance as well as critical evaluation. The truth is that we no longer have to be so tentative in proposing difficult writers as people who are to be taken seriously, for our era has more than caught up with their innovations.

It may be that posterity has already decided that James Joyce and William Faulkner, to take two prominent examples, were finer writers than Gertrude Stein. But, for the sake of argument, we could suggest that *The Making of Americans, Tender Buttons,* and *Four Saints in Three Acts* are just as completely realized works of art — *given their conventions* — as *Ulysses* or *The Sound and the Fury.* That most people find themselves going back more frequently to reread Joyce and Faulkner may suggest only that our attention spans and literary expectations have been conditioned more to the accretion of "meanings" in fictional creation than to the subtraction of them. Arid in meaning though much of her writing may seem, Stein attains at her best a stylistic purity that is rare in any art form. *The Making of Americans,* for instance, is as sustained an act of concentration and stylistic consistency as any long novel in English.

The fact that the present decade has witnessed the steady rise in all the arts of works that explore the possibilities of nonsense makes it easier for us to see now the nature of Stein's achievement in its totality. The recent reprinting of almost all her books — ones that existed before only in rare original editions — corresponds to something of a hidden cultural need. The great success of "Four Americans in Paris" — the exhibition of paintings from the collections of Gertrude, Leo, Sarah, and Michael Stein that toured the United States in 1971[3] — shows the continuing appeal this romantic family retains even for those who have never read a line of experimental prose. This fact had already been recognized by educational television on which an excellent documentary of Gertrude Stein's life was shown to millions of viewers. There have been recent productions of a number of Stein's dramas, as well as Leon Katz's adaptation of *The Making of Americans*, which opened in New York in December 1972. There is, at present, no waning in the recent spate of interest.

That Stein continued to develop new styles throughout her long career, composing some of her most important works at the very end of her life, gives at least a partial lie to F. Scott Fitzgerald's famous contention that "There are no second acts in American lives."[4] Stein's life had at least four or five acts; and, when we think of the great number of American writers who have had trouble sustaining themselves creatively after their early successes (Fitzgerald and Melville come immediately to mind), her consistency is an achievement in itself. It seems clear that the energies of Modernism made this possible: the willingness to see writing as primarily a continuous exercise in compositional problem solving, along with a constant search for new styles so as to avoid repeating oneself.

It would be delusory, however, to suggest that Stein's most innovative works will ever be read widely. Few readers will ever be willing to give *The Making of Americans* and *Tender Buttons* the kind of sustained attention those books require, and it is difficult to insist that they should. Most readers will still discover their Stein in *The Autobiography of Alice B. Toklas* and *Three Lives*; and these important works will, no doubt, continue to be read widely. Stein's achievements in the drama are being increasingly recognized and admired; and, as her notebooks are published and as more critics discuss the writings in the Yale Edition of her previously unpublished works, she will assume greater and greater importance in any serious consideration of the meaning of twentieth-century literature — and she will do so in genuine critical terms, not simply in notoriety — for to reject Stein any longer is to reject Modernism. While this rejection may be a luxury that some people will continue to permit themselves, it is one that no serious reader can afford to indulge. To deal properly with modern letters, we must face the work of Gertrude Stein head on, in both its intrinsic and its cultural significance. She is too large a fact to be ignored any longer.

Notes and References

Preface

1. John Malcolm Brinnin, *The Third Rose: Gertrude Stein and Her World* (Boston, 1959), p. xiv.
2. Richard Bridgman, *Gertrude Stein in Pieces* (New York, 1970), pp. 365 - 85.

Chapter One

1. Gertrude Stein, *Everybody's Autobiography* (New York, 1937), p. 50.
2. Leo Stein, *Journey into the Self* (New York, 1950), p. 230. He speaks of her "pretentious simplicity."
3. See Sherwood Anderson, "Introduction," in *Geography and Plays* (Boston, 1922).
4. *The Autobiography of Alice B. Toklas* (New York, n.d.), p. 219. (The original edition was published in 1933.)
5. See Thornton Wilder, "Introduction," *Four in America* (New Haven, 1947); and Virgil Thomson, "Preface," *Bee Time Vine* (New Haven, 1953).
6. Donald Sutherland, *Gertrude Stein: A Biography of Her Work* (New Haven, 1951).
7. B. L. Reid, *Art by Subtraction: A Dissenting Opinion of Gertrude Stein* (Norman, Oklahoma, 1958).
8. Kingsley Widmer, *The Literary Rebel* (Carbondale and Edwardsville, Illinois, 1965), p. 208.
9. John Malcolm Brinnin, *The Third Rose: Gertrude Stein and Her World* (Boston, 1959).
10. Michael J. Hoffman, *The Development of Abstractionism in the Writings of Gertrude Stein* (Philadelphia, 1965).
11. Allegra Stewart, *Gertrude Stein and the Present* (Boston, 1967).

12. Norman Weinstein, *Gertrude Stein and the Literature of Modern Consciousness* (New York, 1970).

13. Richard Bridgman, *Gertrude Stein in Pieces* (New York, 1970).

14. James Mellow, *Charmed Circle: Gertrude Stein & Company* (New York, 1974).

15. The growing acceptance of Gertrude Stein into the canon of "respectable" authors is well demonstrated by two facts: (1) a growing number of Ph.D. theses written on her work (a traditional indicator of literary respectability); and (2) a remarkable number of recent popular biographies, including three "juveniles" (see selected Bibliography) and James Mellow's celebrated *Charmed Circle* which was nominated for a National Book Award. Articles appear now on her in *PMLA* and *American Literature* with some frequency.

16. Gertrude Stein and Leon M. Solomons, "Normal Motor Automatism," *Psychological Review* 3 (September 1896), 492 - 512; and Gertrude Stein, "Cultivated Motor Automatism," *Psychological Review* 5 (May 1898), 295 - 306. See also "Gertrude Stein in the Psychology Laboratory," which appears in the Appendix to *The Development of Abstractionism in the Writings of Gertrude Stein.*

17. *The Autobiography of Altce B. Toklas,* pp. 82 - 83.

18. Elizabeth Sprigge, *Gertrude Stein: Her Life and Work* (New York, 1957), p. 13.

19. *Lectures in America* (Boston, 1957), pp. 137 - 38. (The original edition was published in 1935.)

20. *Things as They Are* (Pawlet, Vermont, 1950). *Q. E. D.* was published recently in *Fernhurst, Q. E. D., and Other Early Writings* (New York, 1971). This edition uses the original title and contains an unemended text.

21. Dreiser begins *Sister Carrie* with a discussion of both Drouet and Carrie as representatives of particular psychological and sociological types. Steffens speaks in his *Autobiography* of going to Germany as a young man to study psychology in order to discover at last the typological basis of all human personality.

22. This by now apocryphal statement is quoted in many sources, including *The Autobiography of Alice B. Toklas.*

23. Hoffman, pp. 28 - 29.

24. James Joyce, *A Portrait of the Artist as a Young Man* (New York, 1964), p. 215.

25. Hoffman, p. 29.

Chapter Two

1. Gertrude Stein, *Things as They Are* (Pawlet, Vt., 1950). This edition of 516 copies was printed with some names and phrases changed. In the trade edition published by Liveright, the text follows Stein's manuscript. The

Sophie Neathe of the 1950 edition is now Mabel Neathe, reflecting the original model for that character, a John Hopkins friend named Mabel Haynes.

2. In an excellent unpublished doctoral dissertation ("The First Making of *The Making of Americans*," Columbia University, 1963), Leon Katz examines the biographical and intellectual backgrounds of all of Stein's writing to 1908. Katz is the first scholar to have been given complete access to the voluminous collection of Stein notebooks in the Yale Collection of American Literature. As a result of his discoveries, two things become obvious. One is that the notebooks must eventually be published. The other is that all our estimates of Stein's early career will have to be revised in the light of the evidence contained in Katz's dissertation and in the notebooks themselves.

The other members of the *Q. E. D.* triangle were fellow students with Stein at Johns Hopkins, Mabel Haynes and May Bookstaver, the latter being the model for Helen Thomas and the former for Mabel Neathe. It was during the depression following her unsuccessful love affair with May Bookstaver that Gertrude Stein wrote *Q. E. D.*, never fully intending to publish it. Alice Toklas confirmed that "the dialogue . . . is based almost wholly on the correspondence between Miss Bookstaver and Miss Stein, which Miss Stein had before her and followed closely during the writing of the book. The correspondence of dialogue and letters cannot be verified. When the novel came to light in 1932, and Miss Toklas discovered its biographical connection, she destroyed all Miss Bookstaver's letters in a passion.' " (Katz, p. 16n)

Katz has summarized some of his findings in the "Introduction" to *Fernhurst, Q. E. D., and Other Early Writings*. It is to be hoped that he will use his considerable knowledge of the Stein materials in a full-length work, perhaps a biography.

3. Brinnin, *The Third Rose*, p. 45.

4. Phillip Rahv, "Notes on the Decline of Naturalism," in *Image and Idea* (Norfolk, Connecticut, 1957).

5. *The Autobiography of Alice B. Toklas*, p. 78.

6. *Fernhurst, Q. E. D., and Other Early Writings*, p. 121. Other page references appear in the text.

7. Hoffman, p. 56.

8. This has been reprinted in *Motor Automatism*, ed. Robert A. Wilson (New York, 1969), which includes both of Stein's articles from the *Psychological Review*.

9. "Cultivated Motor Automatism," 299.

10. *The Making of Americans* (Paris, 1925), p. 3.

11. Hoffman, p. 54.

12. See Chapter 4 of E. M. Forster, *Aspects of the Novel* (New York, 1927).

13. *Three Lives* was published in 1909 by the Grafton Press.

14. *The Autobiography of Alice B. Toklas*, p. 34.

15. In "A Transatlantic Interview 1946" Gertrude Stein said,

Everything I have done has been influenced by Flaubert and Cézanne, and this gave me a new feeling about composition. Up to that time composition had consisted of a central idea, to which everything else was an accompaniment and separate but was not an end in itself, and Cézanne conceived the idea that in composition one thing was as important as another thing. Each part is as important as the whole, and that impressed me enormously, and it impressed me so much that I began to write *Three Lives* under this influence and this idea of composition and I was more interested in composition at that moment, this background of word-system, which had come to me from this reading that I had done, I was obsessed by this idea of composition, and the Negro story ("Melanctha" in *Three Lives*) was a quintessence of it.

See *A Primer for the Gradual Understanding of Gertrude Stein,* ed. Robert Bartlett Haas (Los Angeles, 1971), p. 15.

16. *Three Lives* (New York, n.d.), p. 239. All other page references to *Three Lives* appear in the text.

17. Hoffman, pp. 71 - 72.

18. See Brinnin, pp. 120 - 21.

19. Donald Sutherland, *Gertrude Stein: A Biography of Her Work,* p. 44.

20. This claim has been made by both Leo Stein and Richard Bridgman. See Bridgman's "Melanctha," *American Literature* 33 (November 1961), 354.

Chapter Three

1. The first edition of *The Making of Americans* was published by Robert McAlmon's Contact Editions (Paris, 1925). It was published in New York the following year by Albert & Charles Boni.

2. Edmund Wilson, *Axel's Castle* (New York, 1931), p. 239.

3. *The Making of Americans* (New York, 1934).

4. Harvest Books reprinted the shorter version of *The Making of Americans* in paperback (1965), and Something Else Press the long version the following year.

5. *The Making of Americans* ("An Opera and a Play"), adapted by Leon Katz (New York, 1973). The opera was performed in the fall of 1972 at the Judson Poets' Theater, under the direction of Lawrence Kornfeld. The musical score is by Al Carmines.

6. Parts of *The Making of Americans* were first published in 1924 in Ford Madox Ford's *transatlantic review* through the agency of Ernest Hemingway. This brought the book to the attention of McAlmon who published the entire book a year later.

7. Leon Katz, "The First Making of *The Making of Americans,*" unpublished PhD dissertation (Columbia University, 1963). For most of the dates and background information I have depended on Katz.

8. In *Fernhurst, Q. E. D., and Other Early Writings.* Further page references are to this edition.

9. See above, Chapter 2.

10. Katz, p. 45.

11. See Bridgman, *Gertrude Stein in Pieces,* p. 82.

12. Bridgman, p. 79.

13. See "Fernhurst," in *Fernhurst, Q. E. D., and Other Early Writings* (New York, 1971).

14. Bridgman, pp. 85 - 86.

15. George Knox, "The Great American Novel: Final Chapter," *American Quarterly* 21 (Winter 1969), 679. Knox calls *The Making of Americans* a "super-spoof of the tradition."

16. *The Making of Americans* (Paris, 1925), pp. 190 - 91. All other page references to *The Making of Americans* appear in the text. The pagination of the recent Something Else Press reprint is the same.

17. Hoffman, p. 105.

18. See George Haines, IV, "Gertrude Stein and Composition," *Sewanee Review* 57 (Summer 1949), 413.

19. See Eliot's much anthologized essay, "Tradition and the Individual Talent," in *Selected Essays* (London, 1951), pp. 13 - 22.

20. See "The Buried Narrative" in Katz, pp. 159 - 94.

21. Gertrude Stein, *Lectures in America,* p. 138.

22. Katz, pp. 85 - 86.

23. Leon Katz has suggested that the "main interest" of the novel is "the conflicts, tensions, and solid justifications of bourgeois marriage" (196). This type of interest is not surprising to those who know how strongly Stein — like Adele in *Things as They Are* — defended most middle-class values. In addition, as Katz points out, Stein was deeply influenced by Otto Weininger's *Sex and Character,* an attempt by a Viennese philosopher and psychologist to erect a typological structure, according to sexual characteristics, that would include all of humanity.

24. Donald Sutherland, *Gertrude Stein: A Biography of Her Work,* p. 61.

Chapter Four

1. *The Making of Americans,* p. 479.

2. Geoffrey Brereton, *A Short History of French Literature* (London, 1954), pp. 77 - 78.

3. *Lectures in America,* p. 148.

4. *A Long Gay Book,* in *Matisse Picasso and Gertrude Stein* (Paris, 1932), p. 16. Page references appear in the text. A recent paperback reprint of *GMP* was published by Something Else (New York, 1972).

5. See the following quotation from an unpublished essay by Gertrude Stein, "American Language and Literature," which is in the Yale Collection of American Literature, Beinecke Library:

I found myself plunged into a vortex of words, burning words, cleansing words, liberating words, feeling words, and the words were all ours and it was enough that we held them in our hands to play with them; whatever you can play with is yours, and this was the beginning of knowing; of all American knowing, that it could play and play with words and the words were all ours all ours.

6. See the following statement by Desmond McCarthy and Roger Fry, as quoted in Alfred H. Barr, Jr., *Matisse: His Art and His Public* (New York, 1951), p. 111:

Primitive art, like the art of children, consists not so much in an attempt to represent what the eye perceives, as to put a line round a mental conception of the object. Like the work of the primitive artist, the pictures children draw are often extraordinarily expressive. But what delights them is to find they are acquiring more and more skill in producing a deceptive likeness of the object itself. Give them a year of drawing lessons and they will probably produce results which will give the greatest satisfaction to them and their relations; but to the critical eye the original expressiveness will have vanished completely from their work.

7. *Two: Gertrude Stein and Her Brother* (New Haven, 1951), pp. 2 - 3. Other page references appear in the text.

8. Types 1, 2, 4, and 5 were first presented in Hoffman, p. 163.

9. A few of the other titles are "Jenny, Helen, Hannah, Paul and Peter," "Four Protégés," and "Flirting at the Bon Marché."

10. *Selected Writings of Gertrude Stein*, ed. Carl Van Vechten (New York, 1962), pp. 333 - 35.

11. *Portraits and Prayers* (New York, 1934), p. 40.

12. Katz, "The First Making of *The Making of Americans*," p. 124.

13. *Geography and Plays*, p. 157. Other page references appear in the text.

14. *Portraits and Prayers*, p. 98.

15. Ibid., p. 211

16. See Alex Preminger, et al., *Princeton Encyclopedia of Poetry and Poetics* (Princeton, New Jersey, 1965), pp. 249 - 50.

17. Ibid., p. 212.

18. Katz, p. 297.

19. Allegra Stewart, p. 72.

20. *Selected Writings*, p. 465. This is the most easily available edition of *Tender Buttons*. Other page references appear in the text.

21. Julian Sawyer, "Descriptions of Gertrude Stein," in *Gertrude Stein, A Bibliography* (New York, 1941), pp. 16 - 17.

22. See particularly the analyses by Bridgman, Hoffman, Stewart, and Sutherland.

23. Stein discusses her concepts of human nature and human mind most fully in *The Geographical History of America* (New York, 1936).

24. *Four in America* (New Haven, 1947), p. xv.

25. These "data" are central concerns of both Henri Bergson and William James. See especially Bergson's *Time and Free Will*, trans. F. L. Pogson (London, 1910). This book was originally published in 1889 as *Essai sur les données immédiates de la conscience.*

Chapter Five

1. Stein defines "landscape" in *Lectures in America*, p. 125, as follows:

The landscape has its formation and as after all a play has to have formation and be in relation one thing to the other thing and as the story is not the thing as any one is always telling something then the landscape not moving but being always in relation, the trees to the hills the hills to the fields the trees to each other any piece of it to any sky and then any detail to any other detail, the story is only of importance if you like to tell or like to hear a story but the relation is there anyway. And of that relation I wanted to make a play and I did, a great number of plays.

2. *Lectures in America*, p. 119:

I came to think that since each one is that one and that there are a number of them each one being that one, the only way to express this thing each one being that one and there being a number of them knowing each other was in a play. And so I began to write these plays. And the idea in What Happened, A Play was to express this without telling what happened, in short to make a play the essence of what happened.

3. Perhaps the best general discussion of Stein's plays appears in Bruce F. Kawin, *Telling It Again and Again* (Ithaca, New York, 1972).

4. *Geography and Plays*, p. 210.

5. *Selected Operas and Plays of Gertrude Stein*, ed. John Malcolm Brinnin (Pittsburgh, 1970).

6. Virgil Thomson, *Capital Capitals*, in *New Music*, 20 (April 1947).

7. Radio Corporation of America, Victor Red Seal Recording, LM-2756.

8. Bridgman, *Gertrude Stein in Pieces*, p. 176. Further page references appear in the text.

9. T. S. Eliot, "Burnt Norton," line 61.

10. *Selected Operas and Plays*, ed. Brinnin, p. 41.

11. *Four Saints in Three Acts* (New York, 1948).

12. Allegra Stewart, *Gertrude Stein and the Present*, pp. 141 - 87.

13. *Selected Operas and Plays*, ed. Brinnin, pp. 239 - 46.

14. "Why I Like Detective Stories," *Harper's Bazaar* [London], 17 (November 1937), 70.

15. See Carl Van Vechten, "How Many Acts Are There In It?," in *Last Operas and Plays* (New York, 1949), p. xiii.

16. *The Mother of Us All* (New York: Music Press, n.d.).

17. *Selected Operas and Plays*, ed. Brinnin, p. 202.

Chapter Six

1. *A Novel of Thank You* (New Haven, 1958), p. ix. Other page references appear in the text.
2. Bridgman, *Gertrude Stein in Pieces,* pp. 172 - 73.
3. *Lucy Church Amiably* (Paris, 1930).
4. Brinnin, p. 294. Further page references appear in the text.
5. Donald Sutherland, *Gertrude Stein: A Biography of Her Work*, p. 143.
6. *Blood on the Dining-Room Floor* was first published with a Foreword by Donald Gallup by the Banyan Press (Pawlet, Vermont, 1948).
7. Erich Neumann, *The Origins and History of Consciousness* (Princeton, 1954).
8. A recent paperback reprint of *The World Is Round* was published by Avon (1972).
9. The original version of *Ida, A Novel* was "Ida," a sketch composed in 1937 and published the following year in London in *The Boudoir Companion*, ed. Page Cooper, p. 31.
10. *Mrs. Reynolds and Five Earlier Novelettes 1931 - 1942* (New Haven, 1952), with a Foreword by Lloyd Frankenberg.
11. *Brewsie and Willie* (New York, 1946).

Chapter Seven

1. See, for example, Frederick J. Hoffman, *The Twenties* (New York, 1955), pp. 224 - 26.
2. There is a recording of Stein reading from *The Making of Americans,* "A Valentine to Sherwood Anderson," "If I Told Her," "Matisse," and "Madame Recamier," on Caedmon TC-1050 (1956). This recording was taken from tapes made during the American lecture tour.
3. An amusing anecdote in *The Autobiography of Alice B. Toklas,* pp. 232 - 33, concerns the composition of this lecture. Other page references to *The Autobiography* appear in the text.
4. "Composition as Explanation," in *What Are Masterpieces* (New York, 1970), pp. 25 - 26. Other page references appear in the text.
5. *Lectures in America* (New York, 1935). All page references in the text refer to the paperback reprint (Boston, 1957).
6. *Gertrude Stein in Pieces,* p. 243.
7. See Rosalind Miller, *Gertrude Stein: Form and Intelligibility* (New York, 1949).
8. *The Geographical History of America* (New York, 1936). Page references appear in the text.
9. *Four in America* was not published until after Stein's death (New Haven, 1947).
10. *Narration* was published soon after the lectures were given (Chicago, 1935). Page references appear in the text.

11. *transition*, 23, Pamphlet no. 1 (February 1935).

12. Alice Toklas, *What Is Remembered* (New York, 1963).

13. George Wickes, *Americans in Paris* (New York, 1969).

14. Fernande Olivier, *Picasso et Ses Amis* (Paris, 1933).

15. Roger Shattuck, *The Banquet Years: The Arts in France, 1885 - 1918* (New York, 1958).

16. See Donald Gallup, ed., *The Flowers of Friendship: Letters Written to Gertrude Stein* (New York, 1953), p. 165, for the following excerpt from a letter to Stein that shows the young Hemingway's adulatory tone toward his teacher before their falling out: "It used to be easy before I met you. I certainly was bad, gosh, I'm awfully bad now but it's a different kind of bad . . ." (15 August 1924).

17. Ernest Hemingway, *A Moveable Feast* (New York, 1964). The two relevant chapters are called "Miss Stein Instructs" and " 'Une Génération Perdue.' "

18. Donald Sutherland, "Alice and Gertrude and Others," *Prairie Schooner*, 45 (Winter 1971 - 1972), 284 - 99.

19. James Mellow, *Charmed Circle: Gertrude Stein & Company* (New York, 1974), p. 458.

20. *Everybody's Autobiography* (New York, 1937). Other page references appear in the text.

21. The French edition of *Picasso* was published in 1938 by the Librairie Fleury, and the English version by B. T. Batsford, Ltd. (London, 1938). Page references are to the American paperback reprint (Boston, 1959).

22. *Paris France* (London, 1940). Page references are to the paperback reprint (New York, 1970).

23. *Wars I Have Seen* (New York, 1945). Page references appear in the text.

Chapter Eight

1. Brinnin, *The Third Rose*, p. xiv.

2. See Sherwood Anderson, "Introduction," in *Geography and Plays* (Boston, 1922).

3. The catalogue written for that exhibition — *Four Americans in Paris* (New York, 1971) — contains a number of interesting essays on Stein and her family as well as passable reproductions of almost all the paintings owned by Michael, Sarah, Leo, and Gertrude Stein.

4. See the notes to F. Scott Fitzgerald, *The Last Tycoon*, ed. Edmund Wilson (New York, 1941), p. 163.

Selected Bibliography

PRIMARY SOURCES

The following is a chronological list of all of Stein's books with the date of their first publication. Almost every one of these is now in print, either in hardcover or paperback.

1. Chief Works

Three Lives. New York: Grafton Press, 1909.

Tender Buttons. New York: Claire Marie Press, 1914.

Geography and Plays. Boston: Four Seas Press, 1922. Foreword by Sherwood Anderson.

The Making of Americans. Paris: Contact Editions, 1925.

Composition as Explanation. London: Hogarth Press, 1926.

Useful Knowledge. New York: Payson & Clarke, 1928.

Lucy Church Amiably. Paris: Plain Edition, 1930.

Before the Flowers of Friendship Faded Friendship Faded. Paris: Plain Edition, 1931.

How to Write. Paris: Plain Edition, 1931.

Operas and Plays. Paris: Plain Edition, 1932.

Matisse Picasso and Gertrude Stein with Two Shorter Stories. Paris: Plain Edition, 1933.

The Autobiography of Alice B. Toklas. New York: Harcourt, Brace, 1933.

Four Saints in Three Acts. New York: Random House, 1934.

Portraits and Prayers. New York: Random House, 1934.

Lectures in America. New York: Random House, 1935.

Narration. Chicago: University of Chicago Press, 1935. Introduction by Thornton Wilder.

The Geographical History of America. New York: Random House, 1936. Introduction by Thornton Wilder.

Everybody's Autobiography. New York: Random House, 1937.

Picasso. London: B. T. Batsford, 1938.
The World Is Round. New York: William R. Scott, 1939.
Paris France. London: B. T. Batsford, 1940.
What Are Masterpieces. Los Angeles: Conference Press, 1940. Foreword by Robert Bartlett Haas.
Ida, A Novel. New York: Random House, 1941.
Wars I Have Seen. New York: Random House, 1945.
Brewsie and Willie. New York: Random House, 1946.
The Gertrude Stein First Reader and Three Plays. Dublin: Maurice Fridberg, 1946.
Four in America. New Haven: Yale University Press, 1947. Introduction by Thornton Wilder.
Blood on the Dining-Room Floor. Pawlet, Vermont: Banyan Press, 1948. Foreword by Donald Gallup.
Last Operas and Plays. New York: Rinehart & Co., 1949. Introduction by Carl Van Vechten.
Things As They Are. Pawlet, Vermont: Banyan Press, 1950.

2. The Yale Edition of the Unpublished Writings of Gertrude Stein

Two: Gertrude Stein and Her Brother and Other Early Portraits (1908 - 1912). New Haven: Yale University Press, 1951. Foreword by Janet Flanner.
Mrs. Reynolds and Five Earlier Novelettes (1931 - 1942). New Haven: Yale University Press, 1952. Foreword by Lloyd Frankenberg.
Bee Time Vine and Other Pieces (1913 - 1927). New Haven: Yale University Press, 1953. Preface and notes by Virgil Thomson.
As Fine As Melanctha (1914 - 1930). New Haven: Yale University Press, 1954. Foreword by Natalie Clifford Barney.
Painted Lace and Other Pieces (1914 - 1937). New Haven: Yale University Press, 1955. Introduction by Daniel-Henry Kahnweiler.
Stanzas in Meditation and Other Poems (1929 - 1933). New Haven: Yale University Press, 1956. Preface by Donald Sutherland.
Alphabets and Birthdays. New Haven: Yale University Press, 1957. Introduction by Donald Gallup.
A Novel of Thank You. New Haven: Yale University Press, 1958. Introduction by Carl Van Vechten.

3. Collected Editions

Selected Writings of Gertrude Stein. Edited with an introduction by Carl Van Vechten, with an essay on Stein by F. W. Dupee. New York: Modern Library, 1962.
Gertrude Stein: Writings and Lectures 1909 - 1945. Edited by Patricia Meyerowitz. London: Peter Owen, 1967. Introduction by Elizabeth Sprigge.

Gertrude Stein on Picasso. Edited by Edward Burns. New York: Liveright, 1970. Afterword by Leon Katz and Edward Burns.

Fernhurst, Q. E. D., and Other Early Writings. New York: Liveright, 1971. Introduction by Leon Katz.

A Primer for the Gradual Understanding of Gertrude Stein. Edited by Robert Bartlett Haas. Los Angeles: Black Sparrow Press, 1971. Good introductory anthology of Stein's writing.

Sherwood Anderson/Gertrude Stein: Correspondence and Personal Essays. Edited by Ray Lewis White. Chapel Hill, North Carolina: University of North Carolina Press, 1972. Good collection of the authors' mutual correspondence and essays to and about one another.

The Making of Americans, An Opera and a Play from the Novel by Gertrude Stein. Adapted by Leon Katz. Barton & Brownington; Something Else Press, 1973.

Reflections on the Atomic Bomb. Edited by Robert Bartlett Haas. Los Angeles: Black Sparrow Press, 1973.

How Writing is Written. Edited by Robert Bartlett Haas. (Volume 2 of the Previously Uncollected Writings of Gertrude Stein.) Los Angeles: Black Sparrow Press, 1974.

4. Manuscripts

The great repository of Stein materials is at the Collection of American Literature, in the Beinecke Rare Book Library, Yale University. All the manuscripts of any significance have now been published with the exception of her letters and her notebooks. There seem to be no plans at present to publish the letters, but an edition of the notebooks is being prepared by Leon Katz and will be published by Liveright.

SECONDARY SOURCES

1. Bibliographies

HAAS, ROBERT BARTLETT and DONALD CLIFFORD GALLUP. *A Catalogue of the Published and Unpublished Writings of Gertrude Stein.* New Haven: Yale University Press, 1941. Good, but must be supplemented by checklist in Bridgman.

SAWYER, JULIAN. *Gertrude Stein. A Bibliography.* New York: Arrow Editions, 1941, Superseded, but contains an interesting introduction.

————. "Gertrude Stein (1874 -): A Checklist Comprising Critical and Miscellaneous Writings about Her Work, Life and Personality from 1913 - 1942," *Bulletin of Bibliography,* 17 (January-April 1943), 211 - 12; 18 (May-August 1943), 11 - 13.

————. "Gertrude Stein: A Bibliography 1941 - 1948," *Bulletin of Bibliography,* 19 (May-August 1948), 152 - 56; (September-December 1948), 183 - 87. Both of these are good but incomplete coverages of their periods. Very much out of date.

WILSON, ROBERT A. *Gertrude Stein: A Bibliography.* New York: The Phoenix Bookshop, 1974. The best and most complete bibliography of Stein's writings. Some inaccuracies.

2. PhD Theses

BLOMME, GAYLE CAMPBELL BARNES. "Gertrude Stein's Concepts of the Self and Her Literary Characters." University of Michigan, 1973. Competent study, with some psychological orientation.

GARVIN, HARRY. "Gertrude Stein: A Study of Her Theory and Practice." University of Michigan, 1949. Begins well; the last half is very thin.

HOFFMAN, MICHAEL J. "The Development of Abstractionism in the Writings of Gertrude Stein to 1913." University of Pennsylvania, 1963. The first version of *The Development of Abstractionism in the Writings of Gertrude Stein.*

KATZ, LEON. "The First Making of *The Making of Americans:* A Study Based on Gertrude Stein's Notebooks and Early Versions of her Novel (1920 - 28)." Columbia University, 1963. One of the better pieces ever written about Stein. Should be published.

LEACH, WILFORD. "Gertrude Stein and the Modern Theatre." University of Illinois, 1956. Interesting, but now a little dated.

LOWE, FREDERICK W., Jr. "Gertrude's Web: A Study of Gertrude Stein's Literary Relationships." Columbia University, 1957. Has a lot of useful information about who came and went at Stein's salon.

MCMILLAN, SAMUEL H. "Gertrude Stein, the Cubists, and the Futurists." University of Texas, 1964. A good subject, but it does not develop many new insights.

ROE, NANCY ELLEN. "Gertrude Stein: Rhetoric and the 'Modern Composition.'" University of Michigan, 1971. Well-done look at Stein's rhetorical structures.

3. Articles

ALKON, PAUL K. "Visual Rhetoric in the *The Autobiography of Alice B. Toklas.*" *Critical Inquiry* 1 (June 1975), 849 - 81. Stimulating, unusual point of view on *The Autobiography.*

FENDELMAN, EARL. "Happy Birthday, Gertrude Stein." *American Quarterly* 27 (March 1975), 99 - 107. Excellent retrospective overview.

FITZ, L. T. "Gertrude Stein and Picasso: The Language of Surfaces." *American Literature* 45 (1973), 228 - 37. Good insight into the artistic relationship of the two friends.

GALLUP, DONALD. "A Book Is a Book." *New Colophon* 1 (January 1948), 67 - 80. About the publication and early reception of *Three Lives.* Interesting.

———. "Gertrude Stein and the *Atlantic.*" *Yale University Library Gazette* 28 (January 1954), 109 - 28. Reprints the fascinating correspondence between Stein and Ellery Sedgwick about publishing her work, 1919 - 1933.

————. "The Making of *The Making of Americans.*" *New Colophon* 3 (1950), 54 - 74. Dates the composition; gives an account of the writing of *The Making of Americans.* Must be supplemented by Katz.

GASS, W. H. "Gertrude Stein: Her Escape from Protective Language." *Accent* 18 (Autumn 1958), 233 - 44. Excellent at setting matters straight in relation to Reid's *Art by Subtraction.*

RIDING, LAURA. "The New Barbarian and Gertrude Stein." *transition* (June 1927), 153 - 68. The first long study of Stein, and still interesting.

SCHMITZ, NEIL. "Gertrude Stein as Post-Modernist: The Rhetoric of Tender Buttons." *Journal of Modern Literature* 3 (July 1974), 1203 - 18. One of the best essays on *Tender Buttons.*

STEWART, ALLEGRA. "The Quality of Gertrude Stein's Creativity." *American Literature* 28 (January 1957), 488 - 506. Excellent in tracing Stein's intellectual backgrounds.

STEWART, LAWRENCE D. "Gertrude Stein and the Vital Dead." *Mystery and Detection Annual* 1 (1972), 102 - 23. Good study of Stein as a writer of "detective stories."

WASSERSTROM, WILLIAM. "The Sursymamericubealism of Gertrude Stein." *Twentieth-Century Literature* 21 (February 1975), 90 - 106. Witty, but too caught up in being clever.

4. Books

BRAQUE, GEORGES et al. *Testimony Against Gertrude Stein. transition*, 23, supplement no. 1, (February 1935). Interesting documentation of the anger caused among some of Stein's acquaintances by *The Autobiography of Alice B. Toklas.*

BRIDGMAN, RICHARD. *The Colloquial Style in America.* New York: Oxford, 1966. Contains a stimulating discussion of Stein's style.

————. *Gertrude Stein in Pieces.* New York: Oxford, 1970. The best book ever on Stein. Indispensable.

BRINNIN, JOHN MALCOLM. *The Third Rose: Gertrude Stein and Her World.* Boston: Little, Brown, 1959. Occasionally too clever; sometimes inaccurate; continually stimulating.

COPELAND, CAROLYN FAUNCE. *Language and Time and Gertrude Stein.* Iowa City, Iowa: University of Iowa, 1975. Clever but slight.

GALLUP, DONALD, ed. *The Flowers of Friendship: Letters Written to Gertrude Stein.* New York: Knopf, 1953. Fascinating collection of letters written to Stein. Reads like a biography.

GREENFELD, HOWARD. *Gertrude Stein: A Biography.* New York: Crown Publishers, 1973. Biography for teenagers. Competent, but not as good as Rogers's.

HOBHOUSE, JANET. *Everybody Who Was Anybody: A Biography of Gertrude Stein.* A lively book, but nothing new. Excellent photographs and reproductions.

HOFFMAN, FREDERICK J. *Gertrude Stein.* University of Minnesota Pamphlets on American Writers, No. 10. Minneapolis: University of Minnesota, 1961. Best short introduction to Stein.

HOFFMAN, MICHAEL J. *The Development of Abstractionism in the Writings of Gertrude Stein.* Philadelphia: University of Pennsylvania Press, 1965. Detailed account of the progressive development of Stein's characteristic style.

IMBS, BRAVIG. *Confessions of Another Young Man.* New York: Henkle-Yewdale House, 1936. Insignificant personal memoir.

KAWIN, BRUCE F. *Telling It Again and Again.* Ithaca, New York: Cornell University Press, 1972. Contains excellent discussion of time and repetition in Stein, particularly in relation to her plays.

MELLOW, JAMES R. *Charmed Circle: Gertrude Stein & Company.* New York: Praeger, 1974. Best biography. Well written; thoroughly researched; always interesting.

MILLER, ROSALIND. *Gertrude Stein: Form and Intelligibility.* New York: Exposition Press, 1949. Slight as critical study; important because it publishes Stein's Radcliffe themes.

REID, BENJAMIN L. *Art by Subtraction: A Dissenting Opinion of Gertrude Stein.* Norman, Oklahoma: University of Oklahoma Press, 1958. Impassioned, wrongheaded, onesided dismissal of Stein as an artist; but an interesting polemic.

ROGERS, W. G. *Gertrude Stein Is Gertrude Stein Is Gertrude Stein: Her Life and Work.* New York: Thomas Y. Crowell, 1973. A biography for teenagers. Sympathetic and fairly accurate.

———. *When This You See Remember Me: Gertrude Stein in Person.* New York: Rinehart, 1948. Another slight personal memoir.

SIMON, LINDA, ed. *Gertrude Stein: A Composite Portrait.* New York: Avon, 1974. Useful collection of statements by others about Stein.

SPRIGGE, ELIZABETH. *Gertrude Stein: Her Life and Work.* New York: Harper, 1957. Thin, not terribly interesting biography. Superseded by both Brinnin and Mellow.

STEWART, ALLEGRA. *Gertrude Stein and the Present.* Cambridge, Massachusetts: Harvard University Press, 1967. Very interesting, though quirky Jungian analysis of Stein. Sometimes stretches credibility.

SUTHERLAND, DONALD. *Gertrude Stein: A Biography Her Work.* New Haven: Yale University Press, 1951. Brilliant, partisan, infuriating, and indispensable.

TOKLAS, ALICE B. *The Alice B. Toklas Cook Book.* New York: Doubleday, 1954. Lots of fun. Along with interesting recipes, contains a lot of juicy anecdotes.

———. *Staying on Alone: Letters of Alice B. Toklas.* Edited by Edward Burns. New York: Liveright, 1973. Fascinating collection. Better than Alice's memoir.

————. *What Is Remembered.* New York: Holt, Rinehart and Winston, 1963. Gives Alice's version of things. Unfortunately she waited too long to write it.

WEINSTEIN, NORMAN. *Gertrude Stein & the Literature of Modern Consciousness.* New York: Ungar, 1970. Attempt to relate Stein's work to modern theories of language and consciousness. Thin book; of limited usefulness.

WILSON, EDMUND. *Axel's Castle.* New York: Scribners, 1931. The chapter on Stein is the weakest in this important book, but it is still the first major critical study of her work.

WILSON, ELLEN. *They Named Me Gertrude Stein.* New York: Farrar, Straus, and Giroux, 1973. A biography for teenagers. Not as good as the one by Rogers.

Index

DATE DUE

DEMCO 38-297